SEEKING THE LIGHT

Uncovering the Truth about
the Movement of
Spiritual Inner Awareness
and Its Founder John-Roger

By
James R. Lewis

Mandeville Press
Los Angeles, California

Published by Mandeville Press
P.O. Box 513935
Los Angeles, CA 90051-1935

Library of Congress Catalogue Card Number: 98-85096

Printed in the United States of America

ISBN 0-914829-42-4

James R. Lewis, a respected scholar and recognized authority on nontraditional religious movements, approached MSIA in 1994 with a proposal to study the organization. His interest had been piqued by the latest spate of publicity MSIA had received. It had been featured for several weeks, worldwide, in the "Doonesbury" comic strip. Because of the national elections that year, you couldn't turn on the radio, at least in Los Angeles, without hearing references to John-Roger and his alleged connection to one of the area's national candidates.

As the publisher of John-Roger's books, we were enthusiastic about Lewis's proposal. Here was the chance to have a writer and prominent scholar with an international reputation as an expert in cults and nontraditional religions take an objective look at an organization that had been misrepresented and, from our point of view, maligned by the popular media.

We felt it would serve MSIA and the general public for the accurate information to be written by a scholar who understands new religious movements. We were confident that an academic observer would validate that MSIA is a legitimate religion.

Of course, there were some conditions. Dr. Lewis was only willing to do the study if he would be free to access MSIA's records, study its materials, and experience its inner workings. MSIA did agree to that and the result is this book.

We believe the information in this book is important, not just for the Movement of Spiritual Inner Awareness and its members and their families, but for everyone who is interested in the issues of religious persecution, cults, and nontraditional religions.

Judi Goldfader, Publisher
Mandeville Press
P.O. Box 513935
Los Angeles, CA 90051-1935
(323) 737-4055
jrbooks@msia.org
www.mandevillepress.org

TABLE OF CONTENTS

1. Introduction: Dozing into the Light 6

2. Early History and Organization 19

3. Movement Background and Some Religious/
Philosophical Traditions Preceding MSIA 44

4. The Teachings: A Little Soul Travel Goes a Long Way . . 64

5. Stepping onto the Path: Why People Join 92

6. Back to School: Living in the Light 116

   Pictorial History. 141

7. Demographic Profiles of Members and Ex-Members . . 159

8. Ex-Members and the "Cult" Controversy 187

9. Epilog: A Look to the Future 220

   About the Author. 233

   Additional Study and Resource Materials 234

1

INTRODUCTION:
DOZING INTO THE LIGHT

There was a psychiatrist I knew in Los Angeles who, when he has patients who have problems sleeping, has them listen to John-Roger tapes instead of prescribing sleeping pills.

—John-Roger

In the spring of 1991, I was convening a session at a conference on nontraditional religions when someone mentioned that John-Roger Hinkins, a "New Age guru," was in attendance. Scanning the audience, I failed to notice anyone fitting my image of such a personage. The only individual in the room who seemed to have some of the aura of a spiritual master was, I later discovered, a Baptist minister.

When I finally met John-Roger (whom almost everyone in his movement calls J-R), it was easy to see why I had previously failed to notice him: Dressed informally, and otherwise innocuous in appearance, he struck me as an old farmer who had put on his best blue jeans to come to town for supplies. He had also neglected to bring along a retinue of admirers — a sure-fire giveaway for most "New Age guru"-types. Having in the past encountered many ostentatious spiritual leaders whose very presence seemed to demand attention, I was frankly impressed.

The next time I encountered John-Roger was at a meeting in the fall of 1994, during which we finalized arrangements for the present study. I was again struck by J-R's ordinariness: Even at his headquarters, surrounded by members of the Church of the Movement of Spiritual Inner Awareness (MSIA), everything about the man seemed to say, "nobody special."

In our chitchat before the meeting, J-R himself commented on his lack of personal magnetism when he jokingly remarked that "MSIA can't be a cult because a cult is supposed to have a charismatic leader!" This remark seemed to speak directly to the thoughts that were in my mind at the moment. John-Roger was, indeed, one of the least charismatic people I had ever met.

Within a few weeks after this meeting I drove back to Los Angeles to collect some preliminary materials for the study. Like many other contemporary religious movements, MSIA's teachings are propagated via the medium of audio tapes. In fact, very little of what John-Roger has spoken in public seminars across the span of three decades has not been preserved in audio form. Residing as I did some 1-1/2 to 2 hours north of MSIA's Los Angeles center, I was delighted to think that the "road hours" I would be spending on the freeway between L.A. and Santa Barbara could be used productively as part of my research. This initial supposition, however, turned out to be mistaken.

During the course of my first round trip, I dutifully popped in an MSIA tape and began listening. John-Roger has a pleasant, soothing voice. However, except for occasional humorous remarks, his delivery does not particularly arrest the attention. His talks frequently meander around, as if he had just sat down and started speaking about whatever came to his mind. And his teachings, while nice enough, are neither especially original nor otherwise remarkable.

While the novelty of the experience preserved me during my first trip, I was not long into my second journey to L.A. when I found myself starting to nod off in my effort to follow J-R's voice. I was soon forced to eject the tape and listen to a radio station to wake myself up. My next few experiments with MSIA seminar tapes produced the same result — a drowsy feeling as if I had overdosed on antihistamines.

I made a mental note to suggest to the MSIA staff that every tape be labeled with the warning, "Do not listen while operating heavy machinery!" None of the MSIA books I was reading were any more engaging than the tapes.

In the early months of my research, I attended an "Introduction to MSIA" class at a member's home. While this class was fruitful for gathering impressions of Movement participants, I could not help but notice that whenever the facilitator led us in any extended meditation, or whenever he played a J-R tape, almost everyone in the room — new and old members alike — nodded off. "That's nice," I thought, "at least I'm not alone in being bored to tears."

However, my relief at having company in my tedium was not great enough to compensate for the increasing sense of exasperation I was beginning to feel at being unable to understand the draw of MSIA. What in God's name was it that attracted people to this movement? I had studied many other minority religions at close range and, while I might have been profoundly at odds with their practices and doctrines, I could at least understand why someone might be attracted to join. With respect to MSIA, however, every aspect of the Movement seemed bland and unappealing. I can remember coming home to my wife after one particularly narcoleptic meeting, exclaiming, "What the hell is this? What brings people into this movement? Am I going to be bored out of my mind for the next six months of this study?" The prospects looked bleak.

When I confronted members with my frustration, they just laughed: "Jim, it's not what happens at the outer level that's important; it's what happens at the inner levels!" I could at least partially understand their reasoning because of my personal background in meditation and meditative experiences, but what about when participants are constantly falling asleep at meetings? "Oh, that's O.K. Ninety percent of what happens takes place on the inner planes anyway, so even if one falls asleep at a seminar, one still receives most of the spiritual benefits!" This kind of response greeted many of my queries on this topic, and I was perplexed that so many otherwise intelligent people could actually accept such a strange doctrine. Nevertheless I persevered, hoping that eventually something would happen that would make the whole thing come together for me. I was, I felt at the time, searching for some key idea or experience that would make the information I was taking in "jell." Methodologically, I was seeking to understand the religious experience of Movement participants, either in terms of a religious studies approach or in terms of traditional participant-observer research.

Most of the scholars who study minority religions are sociologists. While I often rely upon sociological methodology — to such an extent that I have sometimes described myself as a "born-again" sociologist — my primary training is in the Religionswissenschaft (termed "history of religions" in the English-speaking world) tradition of religious studies. While drawing on insights from sociology, history, anthropology, and so forth, this approach to religion sets itself apart from other academic disciplines by attempting to take religious experiences seriously. Drawing on Edmund Husserl's phenomenological philosophy, historians of religion make a disciplined effort to study the influence of religious experiences in the life of believers without either dismissing such experiences as "merely" psychological or acknowledging that such experiences are linked to some larger, spiritual reality. In other words, to oversimplify, an attempt is made to study the structure and role of such experiences in the religious life without evaluating them as either true or false. What seemed to be missing in my study of MSIA was the understanding of some core experience that would make the teachings come alive as an attractive religious option (whether or not I judged the experience to be ultimately "real").

In the social sciences, particularly in anthropology, the standard approach to field work is participant-observer research. In such an approach, one attempts to set up a dynamic relationship between the role of involved participant and the role of detached observer. When the participant role is properly assumed, one becomes, in effect, a partial, temporary convert who is able to view the world of the people one is studying from the inside (to the extent that this is realistically possible). In terms of this methodology, a large part of my frustration was that, despite my participation in MSIA events and spiritual techniques, I seemed to be fundamentally unable to break out of the role of observer and view the world as an MSIA participant.

The more I spoke with MSIA people, the more it became evident that the key to comprehending the Movement was tied up with the teaching that we are multidimensional beings, existing on many levels of consciousness at the same time. We normally perceive only 10% of reality (the physical world), and the often unperceived 90% (the spiritual worlds) was the arena in which most of whatever happened between John-Roger and his students took place. MSIA teaches that students can learn to become more aware of the other levels of consciousness, ultimately knowing himself/herself as divine. MSIA also teaches that John-Roger and John Morton (J-R's spiritual successor) are "anchors" on the physical plane for the Mystical Traveler Consciousness — a spiritual presence that is able to work simultaneously with many different students. (John-Roger was the anchor for this consciousness from December 1963 through December 1988; John Morton has subsequently anchored the Mystical Traveler Consciousness.) Most of the Traveler's work takes place on the inner levels, guiding students in ways that often do not register on the conscious mind.

As MSIA's full name — the Movement of Spiritual Inner Awareness — indicates, part of the goal of Movement participants is to become more aware of these inner processes. However, as should be evident from the experiences I have thus far described, participants do not seem to be particularly upset if much of their spiritual work takes place while they are "unconscious" or otherwise unaware. As one might anticipate, MSIA explicitly teaches that the Traveler Consciousness works with students during sleep. In fact, one of the explanations I have heard for why J-R's tapes put people to sleep is so that the really important inner work that takes place during a taped seminar can happen without unnecessary interference from the conscious mind. As a statement in one of the Soul Awareness Discourse pamphlets asserts, "You are often not told about the work the Traveler is doing because if you don't know, you can't block it." Sleepers can sometimes become aware of this dimension of the work in dreams, particularly when one encounters the Traveler Consciousness clothed in the image of

J-R or John Morton or some other figure symbolic of wisdom to the dreamer.

One evening, when I was at the peak of frustration with my inability to understand the attraction of MSIA, I had a particularly vivid dream in which John-Roger and I talked about the future of MSIA. We seemed to be discussing a presentation I was going to be doing in a distant town. After I woke up, I had the distinct feeling that the "distant town" represented academia, and that the presentation referred to my published study of MSIA. Did I actually encounter something called the "Mystical Traveler Consciousness" in my dream? MSIA's teachings on such dream encounters are nuanced, and readily acknowledge that meeting a dream figure who appears to be J-R or John Morton can simply be a confused reflection of thoughts one has had during one's daylight consciousness.

Taking my cue from history-of-religions methodology, I was not necessarily interested in determining whether or not my encounter with the dream image of John-Roger was "real" in some ultimate, ontological sense. I was, however, excited finally to have had something like an insider's experience — an experience that made distinct sense in terms of MSIA's ideology and world view. This single dream opened up the Movement in ways I cannot fully articulate. I can only report that, from that day forward, J-R's assertion that, "It doesn't matter what I say; I could just repeat 'ham and eggs, ham and eggs' for a half hour and you'd still get it," made perfect sense. The really important, spiritual work takes place at the inner levels, no matter what is taking place at the outer level.

I looked back at the MSIA books that I had been having difficulty getting into, and they suddenly became lucid and even interesting. Things about MSIA that before had seemed dull and boring suddenly came alive. I was looking at the same data through new eyes. I now had the missing ingredient: the dimension of inwardness. Everything in the Movement was shot through with inwardness and was incomplete and lifeless without this added dimension. I finally had a deep, experiential sense of why people joined MSIA. Some time during their involvement, most Movement participants had had direct, confirming experiences of the Traveler Consciousness operating in their lives, and these experiences formed a core around which the rest of J-R's teachings congealed and made sense.

One of the respondents to a short survey that was mailed to a sampling of current MSIA participants described his attraction to the Movement in a way that perfectly captures the importance of the inner dimension for understanding MSIA:

> *I chose MSIA (which is important, MSIA did not recruit me or proselytize to me) because of my own inner experience, not necessarily the John-Roger seminars or Discourses or the group connection, but because of what I experienced as an individual consciousness. . . . You can read all about MSIA from John-Roger's books and hear about MSIA from John-Roger and John Morton seminars, yet you might not really ever find anything out.*

Or, in the words of another respondent,

> *While there are many opportunities to participate in MSIA . . . the real Movement of Spiritual Inner Awareness, inside of me, comes in my S.E.s [spiritual exercises], my dreams, and in times of introspection and contemplation.*

The first MSIA event I attended after my dream experience was a seminar given by John Morton. I hitched a ride to the event with the Movement's treasurer. On the trip over, I related my dream experience, and explained how that relatively minor experience had opened up my understanding of MSIA. Upon our arrival, I had several stimulating conversations with various people prior to the event itself. For the first time in months, I was relaxed rather than exasperated and took the opportunity simply to enjoy the social interaction. John Morton's talk was preceded by announcements and a little music that set the tone for the gathering. By the time John got up to talk, the room was filled with two or three hundred expectant people.

John Morton is a nice-looking man with a ready smile and a polished manner. He also has a pleasant, but not what I would call a mesmerizing, voice. On that particular night, he began his talk by mentioning that he had been fasting for over a week. I earnestly hope that the lack of food accounts for the spacey, disconnected nature of his presentation which, to my perception, was one of the least engaging lectures I had ever heard. As in many of my earlier experiences with MSIA seminars, I found myself nodding off, uncontrollably drawn into the twilight consciousness between sleeping and wakefulness. Later I had the thought that, if the Movement ever decided to sell a tape of that night's lecture, they should entitle it something like, "MSIA's Answer to Sominex."

After what seemed an eternity, John ended his seminar and walked out of the room. The assembled crowd burst into many separate, highly animated conversations, obviously stimulated by what was to my mind a lackluster presentation. As for myself, I returned to full consciousness and noted with pleasure the response of the audience. While I had gotten nothing out of the lecture myself, the great majority of attendees obviously had, even the ones who, like myself, had nodded off. The event had confirmed the conclusion I was already reaching, namely that what many participants get out of their

MSIA-related experiences is something that cannot be fully grasped at the overt level.

The notion of an inward (and often unconscious) level at which 90% of one's consciousness resides and where spiritual work takes place does much more, however, than explain why it is spiritually okay to fall asleep during seminars. Rather, almost every key idea in MSIA's conceptual scheme is informed, directly or indirectly, by this notion. This is particularly evident in MSIA practices and ideas that appear to be parallel to practices and ideas found in other religious groups.

Take, for example, the practice of creative visualization, which is omnipresent among groups in the metaphysical, occult, New Age family of spiritual groups. Creative visualization is the practice of visualizing a state of affairs one wishes to bring about, with the idea that the simple act of visualization will marshal forces in the spiritual realm that will help create the desired result in the physical. Creative visualization is a kind of "mental magic" that is employed for everything from physical healing (e.g., visualizing a diseased part of the body in full health) to affairs of the heart (e.g., visualizing oneself in a romantic situation with a desired partner).

In terms of its significance within the movement, MSIA's parallel to creative visualization is calling in (or sending) the Light, which is a kind of cross between prayer and visualization. "Light" refers to the same spiritual "energy" that (according to MSIA teachings) Christians call the Holy Spirit. When calling in the Light, one states the problematic situation on which one wishes the Spirit to act and asks for the highest good for the situation and for everyone involved. One need not visualize anything (though, in practice, one often does visualize the wished-for result). One need not, in other words, imagine any specific outcome; rather, one can simply request that the Holy Spirit, in its wisdom, act in ways that are best for the situation — whether or not we are able to grasp the wisdom behind the Light's actions. Furthermore, even when one does imagine a specific result, offering the matter up to the Light "for the highest good" allows the Light to act in ways that can supersede our limited vision of what we think we want.

According to John-Roger, the problem with imagining or asking for something highly specific is that you might actually get what you imagine, as well as the unanticipated consequences of your request. To make the point, J-R has related a number of stories, including the tale of his efforts to attract a new residence:

> *Some time ago I programmed from the universal mind for a house, and the houses started coming forward. I thought I had done everything right, but . . . I found out that I'd neglected to mention the yard, so I had a long house sitting on a little yard and felt cooped up. So I decided I wanted a better yard, but I forgot to program for drainage. So, in the next house, the backyard flooded. I said, "Fine, I want good drainage," and the next house was built beside a big wash. . . .*
>
> *One night I was sitting at home, and I said, "You know, I think the house that's for me is waiting. And, Father, I think you know what I have in mind, so just open my consciousness and direct me to it." I turned it over to God and placed it in the Light for the highest good. About a week later a house came forward that was exactly what I wanted.*

Turning a matter over to the Light with a generic request for the greatest good reflects MSIA's belief in the inner, spiritual dimension of life — that greater reality lying behind the

10% level we normally perceive. The Light acts in ways we often cannot comprehend, in order to bring about the greatest good for all people. As with the spiritual development that takes place during sleep, we do not have to be conscious of the specific processes at work behind the scenes for these process- es to be effective. As a matter of fact, if we knew exactly what was happening, we might be tempted to try to interfere, thus involving ourselves in other people's "karma." Although com- parable, it is clear that sending the Light represents a profound departure from creative visualization.

As a way of delimiting MSIA practices, John-Roger makes a distinction between the Light and what he terms "magnetic light." Magnetic light refers to the impersonal, mechanical energies of the lower spiritual planes that can be manipulated by the human will. Magnetic light is by definition inferior to the Light. The Light proper may be invoked but not manipu- lated by human beings. Creative visualization makes use of the power of magnetic light. By way of contrast, holding some- thing in the Light for the highest good is a way of focusing spiritual energy into a situation and asking (but not com- pelling) God to work His/Her/Its will in the matter. This dis- tinction holds for many other MSIA practices: Though related to, or even derived from, similar practices in other spiritual movements, MSIA practices set themselves apart by allowing room for what in more traditional language we might call the activity of God's Grace (from the 90% level) into our physical lives (the 10% level).

I have laid out the story of my initial efforts to understand MSIA at some length for several reasons. In the first place, while all religious movements speak of visions and revelations that lie beyond the experience of outside observers, I have never before studied a movement for which these experiences played such a central role in understanding both group ideology and individual participation. By relating the tale of my grappling with this issue, I hope that I have thrown some "light" on what participants regard as the most significant aspect of their spirituality.

In the second place, I have attempted to describe my encounter with MSIA in a manner that captures some of the humanity of the Movement. While MSIA may view itself as being directed primarily to the 90% of existence that lies within and beyond, it is also a deeply human venture — a point often lost in outsider accounts of such religious groups.

Finally, academic treatments of other peoples have traditionally been written as if observers of events were machine-like tape recorders who never engaged in human contact with the subjects of their investigations. This mode of presentation misrepresents the actual situations in which information is gathered, and some essential element of understanding is lost when researchers adhere rigidly to this kind of detached style. My approach has been shaped by my background and by certain specific experiences I had in the course of this study. Where relevant, I have made reference to such personal encounters so that readers can have access to some of the experiences which shaped my interpretation of the Movement of Spiritual Inner Awareness.

2

EARLY HISTORY AND
ORGANIZATION

*Since the Law has already been fulfilled, you can only
have guidelines. And those are simple: Out of God
comes all things. God loves all of Its creation. And,
not one soul will be lost.*

—John-Roger

Although John-Roger has often woven stories of his boyhood
and later life into his discourses to underline points he is making, there is no hagiographical literature about a miraculous
birth or a sainted childhood as there is for the founders of
some new religions. Briefly, the bare facts are that John-Roger
was born Roger Hinkins on September 24, 1934, to a
Mormon family in Rains, Utah. Rains is a mining town and
Hinkins' father was a mine foreman. While growing up, the
spiritual-teacher-to-be was more interested in girls and sports
than in spirituality. The only unusual aspect of his childhood
was that he could see "auras," the colorful energy fields that
traditional occultism pictures as surrounding the human body.

He held down a number of jobs, including a short stint in the coal mines. While in college, he worked as a night orderly in the psychiatric ward of a Salt Lake City hospital. Later he held a part-time job as a PBX telephone operator and dispatcher with the Salt Lake City Police Department. After completing a degree in psychology at the University of Utah in 1958, he moved to southern California and eventually took a job teaching English at Rosemead High School.

The turning point of his life occurred in 1963, during what we might today call a near-death experience. While undergoing surgery for a kidney stone, he fell into a nine-day coma. Upon awakening, he found himself aware of a new spiritual personality — "John" — who had superseded/merged with his old personality. After the operation, Hinkins began to refer to himself as "John-Roger," in recognition of his transformed self.

Around this time John-Roger was a seeker exploring a variety of different spiritual teachings, including Eckankar, a Sant Mat-inspired group. Parallels between Eckankar and the Movement of Spiritual Inner Awareness have prompted critics to accuse him of plagiarizing Eckankar. During an interview with J-R, I asked him about his relationship with Paul Twitchell, the founder of Eckankar. His response was:

> *I've been asked, "Were you a student of Eckankar?"*
> *Yeah, if you can consider I was a student of the* Reader's Digest *and* National Geographic *and the Rosicrucians and some other churches all at the same time. I went to some of the churches to see what they did — [I was what they refer to as] a metaphysical tramp. I call those my "meta-fizzle" days because none of those ever worked out.*

No way do I have anything negative with Eckankar. No way. I had a private interview with Twitchell, and he said, "You have the sound [and] the names of the Gods on every realm." I said, "They're all the same God, it's just a different vibration." He said, "You know them?" I said, "Sure I know them." And we discussed the initiation words, and he told me a sampling of his. And I said, "I don't use those, I use the five names." And he said, "Well, I don't think the people will understand the five names." I said, "Not unless you give them to them," because he wasn't going to give it to them. I got a letter a month later that said, "Since you're an initiate of the Sound Current through Eckankar, here's the other information that you're to get." So I looked through the information, and I said, "I don't know why I got this, because I wasn't initiated."

John-Roger thus acknowledges that he studied with Eckankar, but was not, at least according to his own account, ever formally initiated into that organization. As for the parallels between Eckankar and MSIA, John-Roger would probably respond that these similarities result from the fact that truth is one, so why shouldn't they both be saying similar things? This, at least, is how MSIA would view the issue.

Additionally, MSIA's theology is strikingly different in many ways from both Sant Mat's and Eckankar's. One major difference is the position accorded Jesus Christ, who is viewed as the ultimate head of MSIA on this planet. Jesus embodies the Mystical Traveler Consciousness and holds the office of Christ for the earth (roughly like the "presidency" of this planet). John-Roger has also stated that he consciously changed the traditional form of Sant Mat initiatory tones — the "names of the Gods" referred to above — to access and synthesize the cosmic energetic route streams to Soul Transcendence of Eastern and Western mysticism.

After John-Roger's postcoma realization, he did not immediately abandon his career as a high school English teacher. It was not, in fact, until some five years later that he began holding gatherings as an independent spiritual teacher, and not until 1971, that he quit his day job to become a full-time religious leader. How the core group of spiritual seekers came together to hold these first seminars is the foundation story of the Church of the Movement of Spiritual Inner Awareness.

MSIA developed out of a series of six seminars held at the home of Muriel Engle in Santa Barbara, California. The first seminar took place on May 4, 1968. Across the course of six evenings, the audience was modest. Attendance ranged from 13 to 30 persons, depending upon the evening. After Santa Barbara, John-Roger was requested to present seminars in a private home in Thousand Oaks (a community midway between Santa Barbara and Los Angeles). Then they spread across southern California until there was such demand that John-Roger was doing five seminars a week at different homes in different cities. The Church of the Movement of Spiritual Inner Awareness was formally incorporated three years later, in 1971.

Three people organized the first Santa Barbara seminars — Muriel Engle, Jack Reed, and Robert Waterman. All three are involved in MSIA to this day, and Engle and Reed both authored accounts of the beginning of the Movement that were published in *The Movement* newspaper, the organization's periodical (later superseded by *The New Day Herald*). Other source material on the early days can be found in an early MSIA publication, *Across the Golden Bridge*.

Jack Reed's story begins as a young man growing up in the sixties. He left the Air Force Academy in 1965, after attending that institution for a little over a year. After leaving the military, Reed teamed up with a friend in Tucson, and, beginning in late January of 1966, traveled around the country. They often encountered people who shared their spiritual interests.

While attending a week-long metaphysical conference put on by Neva Dell Hunter in Flagstaff, in August of 1966, Reed was introduced to John-Roger by an astrologer friend, Betty Baron. J-R, who immediately impressed Reed as a "weird dude," stood up, shook his hand, and said, "I remember you. You killed me once in Atlantis!" He then added, "You should be very good at transfiguration." Reed says that,

John-Roger and I were immediate friends. In my experience, he was the funniest guy I had ever met, and yet he also had these weird abilities. Despite the clowning, I perceived that he was also very spiritual.

After the conference, John-Roger returned to Rosemead. Reed went to Santa Barbara, where he enrolled as a student at the University of California at Santa Barbara (UCSB). What brought them back together was a bet: Reed and J-R wagered a steak dinner over the sex of the child Reed's brother's wife was expecting. When the boy was born (John-Roger had predicted a girl), Reed drove down to Rosemead to collect. Reed then began visiting J-R on weekends on a regular basis, a custom that continued for the next year and a half.

I went down to see him, and I was also — I was 20 years old then — seeing this girl in La Habra, and it gave me a place to stay. I met several of J-R's students, present and former, because they used to come over and hang out at his place.

I remember his apartment. It was very messy. It was a one-bedroom apartment. There was a surfboard standing in the corner. Dishes weren't usually

> *done [and were stacked] in the sink. And he was into gadgets, so there were electronic gadgets he was trying and stacks of paperwork and stuff. There were no pictures on the wall. I remember very clearly, because I often used to sleep on his couch.*
>
> *On one of my trips down, J-R took me with him to a talk he was giving at Stephen Douglas' metaphysical church in Long Beach. At about the same time, J-R suggested to me that he'd like to give more lectures to broader audiences.*

In the mid-sixties, John-Roger was beginning to come out of the metaphysical closet and do public work in limited ways, such as guest lecturing at spiritual centers and giving Light studies (life pattern/past-life readings that addressed one's spiritual issues). Some of the people who met him during this period later became involved in MSIA.

Reed wanted to set up a lecture for John-Roger at UCSB, and discussed the matter with his friend, Muriel Engle. At the time, Engle worked for UCSB developing that institution's Educational Opportunity Program. She had been involved with alternative, "metaphysical" spirituality for some years and had met Reed through their mutual friend, Neva Dell Hunter. Two years prior to Engle's first meeting with John-Roger, a well-known psychic had predicted that she would meet a young man who would have a major impact on her life, and with whom she would work closely. The clue she had been given by which she would know this person when she met him was "praying hands on a golden disc on a golden chain."

Reed and Engle eventually found a metaphysical center, the Rainbow Temple (actually a private home that had been converted into a center), in downtown Santa Barbara to use for J-R's lecture, which took place in August of 1967. From Reed's description Engle's initial impression was that John-Roger was bright but arrogant. However, she quickly retracted her judgment when she heard him say:

I'm going to present some techniques of expanding your consciousness which will enable you to recognize and understand certain personality traits and characteristics in others; but more important, this will help you see yourself more clearly. I ask only that you keep an open mind; if it works for you, use it. If you have better methods, please share them with me. But if you ever hear me say, "This is the only way," please ask me to sit down.

This humble prologue impressed Engle, who then listened attentively to what J-R had to say. As part of his presentation, John-Roger offered to give the people in attendance short "readings." Engle volunteered first.

His method of handling the vocabulary to fit each one's understanding has always impressed me. He told me I would experience a change of consciousness about the first of the year. I listened but had to admit "nicht verstandt." ("I don't understand.")

John-Roger then attempted to clarify his statement by describing this "change of consciousness" as an initiation. He further observed that it would involve "extensive travel." This later turned out to be a prediction of a flight (at the time unplanned by Engel) to India with the famous yoga teacher Indra Devi to see the holy man Satya Sai Baba.

The evening following the lecture, John-Roger, Reed, and company dined at Engle's house. Following the meal, she commented that she hoped the spaghetti was not too imbalanced starch-wise for someone as sensitive as J-R. He responded with typical humor, asserting that, "We will now have a demon-stration of what the pendulum can do to change the chemical action of Whatever. . . ." He then opened his shirt collar, removed a golden chain over his head, and proceeded to use his medallion like a pendulum — a medallion that was in the form of a "golden disc with praying hands."

When this happened, Engle says, "I froze: I didn't need the sound of trumpets! Every nerve in my body rang in chord. . . ." Reed recalls that,

> *When J-R pulled out the chain with the praying hands, it was a moment where time stood still and there was a presence of Spirit that was overwhelming — like a wind of Spirit had blown in and shimmered; as if we had gone into another realm.*

This remarkable experience did not, however, immediately lead to the cooperative spiritual enterprise that had been pre-dicted in Engle's reading two years prior, and she was "still puzzled" about how she might be working with John-Roger after that unusual evening.

In October, she was offered an opportunity to visit the Ashram of Satya Sai Baba for two weeks, and, on January 4, 1968, flew to India. Engle later reported feeling that she had truly undergone the "change of consciousness" John-Roger had predicted. In her last personal interview with Sai Baba before returning to the United States, she asked him for guid-ance regarding a group of young spiritual seekers who had been meeting regularly at her home:

> *"I need a teacher for the young students coming to my home. I can point them to general information, but we need someone who really knows where each one is, individually." Baba watched me for a*

*moment, then nodded, "Your teacher is at hand; you
will know." That was all!*

She was disappointed by the response, interpreting Sai
Baba's words as indicating that she should rely upon the God
within to fulfill the need for a teacher.

The week following her return, Engle attended a prophecy
class at a town not far from Santa Barbara. Invited to share her
India experience with the class, she made a few introductory
remarks, and then stated, "I really think He [Sai Baba] is the
Christ of our time." This assertion had a dampening effect on
the interest of the group, and she immediately realized that she
had "made a giant blooper." After the class formally conclud-
ed, Engle became engaged in an informal discussion with some
of the people present whom she knew — including John-
Roger, who wanted to hear more about "this great soul you
met in India." After some conversation, John-Roger related to
her that she should have said that Sai Baba "has the Christ
Consciousness," rather than asserting that he "is the Christ."
In the midst of this conversation, Engle recalled Sai Baba's
statement, "Your teacher is at hand; you will know." She
immediately realized that J-R was the teacher for whom she
had asked. Before the evening was over, John-Roger agreed to
hold pilot seminars in Engle's Santa Barbara home — seminars
that became the starting point for MSIA.

A number of people who came to the early seminars drove
from other cities in southern California. As the seminars
became regular, ongoing meetings, these "long-distance"
attendees were able to persuade John-Roger to begin holding
seminars outside of Santa Barbara. This expansion of J-R's
activities continued until he was doing five seminars a week at
different homes in different cities.

Despite the later proliferation of classes, workshops, and
conferences, the home-meeting seminar remained MSIA's core

gathering, fulfilling a role not unlike the Sunday morning meetings of most Christian churches. The format of such seminars was also established in the early days, consisting of a talk by John-Roger, followed by individual "sharings." After the seminar proper, attendees fellowshipped together, perhaps accompanied by tea or some sort of snack.

As the organization expanded until J-R could not personally attend every meeting, a distinction developed between live seminars with John-Roger and taped seminars at which the group listened to a tape of a J-R talk. How the seed of the MSIA organization developed out of the early seminars was related by Engle:

> *The group members didn't need a name; we knew what we were doing and how we were progressing to soul travel and that level of consciousness. But in speaking to others of our activities and development, [we realized that] it was the "others" that seemed to need some identification.*
>
> *All the suggestions were listed, first for the title, then later for the symbol, and each member in each of the seminars (seven at the time) had the opportunity to vote his choice. We voted for weeks until, by the process of elimination, the chosen insignia became well known by the popular acclaim of the first few hundred members of the Movement.*

From these humble beginnings, John-Roger's activities gradually expanded until he had become a full-time spiritual teacher. It was only after several years of steady teaching activity that John-Roger began to formally make people his students by initiating them into the Sound Current.

The Soul Awareness Discourses — the basic lessons that Movement people receive on a monthly basis — originated from the request of some of the early participants for reading material on the teachings, and were derived from seminar transcripts. After the seminars started being taped, each tape would receive a name, based on the topic J-R had discussed that evening. Additionally, a couple of John-Roger's close associates would transcribe the tapes as well as make notes about what was on them.

In response to repeated requests for reading material, these notes were examined for common themes and material brought together from many different seminars to form the basis for printed discourses on particular topics, ranging from "Sending the Light" to "Overcoming Discouragement." The earliest discourses were mimeographed. As MSIA developed, these were periodically revised and expanded, and more advanced levels of the discourses composed for longtime participants.

Nineteen seventy-one was an important threshold, being the year in which the organization was formally incorporated and the first issue of the first Movement periodical, *On the Light Side*, was published. *On the Light Side*, which was not much more than an elaborate newsletter, soon gave way to *The Movement* newspaper, a true alternative magazine that reported on events and personalities in the larger New Age movement, in addition to MSIA activities and concerns.

For reasons that will be discussed more fully in the next chapter, the period of the 1970s was a fruitful decade for the expansion of metaphysical spirituality. An important though little-discussed threshold event that helped set the stage for the spiritual ferment of the seventies was the lowering of immigration barriers to people from Asian countries in 1965. Thus not only were the older occult-metaphysical groups able to experience rapid growth in the wake of an influx of post-countercultural youth, but new Asian teachers were drawing students from this same crop of ex-hippies. Teachers from all of these traditions were interviewed in the pages of *The Movement*.

In more recent years, *The Movement* was succeeded by *The New Day Herald*, an in-house newspaper focused on MSIA news and events. Most of the space in the early *On the Light Side* periodicals was taken up by transcriptions of seminar talks. The content of these transcripts provides a good sense of John-Roger's teachings in the early days. The following citation from the first *On the Light Side* accurately captures J-R's homey, down-to-earth style:

> *First you learn who you are. And when you learn who the real self is, the false images fall away rapidly. The person you thought you were, the religion you thought you were, the philosophy you thought you were may fall away. You may find out that all of these philosophies that you've been adhering to just don't work. But you may be afraid to throw them away because you don't know what will take their place. When you get rid of the things that don't work, you will find the true self. And the true self doesn't have anger or jealousy or greed or lust or avarice. It doesn't have any of these things; it doesn't need them. But the false self has them and needs them and fights for dear life to hang onto them. If you could just once see within the true self, if you could get that image just once in your consciousness for a fraction of a second, you could go on for the rest of your life using that as an inner guiding light.*

This focus on spirituality was, however, supplemented by discussions of some of the more fantastic phenomena one could encounter when treading an esoteric spiritual path. Also, some of the older members I interviewed recalled that many of

John-Roger's seminars presented information about the inner realms. This is related, in part, to a topic that was enjoying considerable attention in the metaphysical subculture of the 1970s — astral projection.

Astral projection, also known as the out-of-body experience (OOBE), refers to the supposed ability of human consciousness to travel outside the physical body. The astral body is said to be an exact replica of the physical body, but more subtle. It is the body that one inhabits immediately after death. It is further said that it is able to detach from the physical body at will, or under certain special circumstances. The astral body remains attached to the physical body via a stream of energy commonly termed the silver cord. It can also spontaneously leave the physical body during sleep, trance, or coma, under the influence of anesthetics or drugs, or as the result of accidents.

The notion of astral projection was popularized by the studies of the British scientist Robert Crookall — who compared hundreds of cases in which people left the physical body and reentered it after traveling unseen in the astral body — and by Sylvan Muldoon and Hereward Carrington, in their books *The Phenomena of Astral Projection* and *The Projection of the Astral Body*. Besides describing the phenomenon, they also reported on some techniques that were said to be effective for experiencing astral projection at will. These were almost all based on a simple, strong desire to project one's own astral body.

Astral projection in the early 1970s was what channeling was to become for the late eighties and, more recently, what angels are for the mid-nineties — a popular fad that almost everyone in the metaphysical subculture had some interest in. While J-R often discussed astral plane experiences, he was also careful to emphasize that MSIA's goal was Soul Transcendence, NOT astral travel. Nevertheless, it is easy to see how the widespread interest in astral projection was the basis for initially bringing certain seekers into contact with John-Roger's teachings. To cite a relevant passage from an early MSIA book, *Inner Worlds of Meditation*:

> *One of the first indicators that you have tapped into the astral consciousness within is that the imagination becomes very fertile. . . . Continuing within, you may start seeing lights — circular lights, triangular lights, square lights, colored lights — and this is all saying that you are moving further within. . . . You may start to see some beautiful, fantastic shapes and designs. If you watch carefully, you will start to see whole scenes appear within the inner vision. It might appear that you're back in King Arthur's court, at his round table. Just observe; it could be one of your past incarnations reflecting through the astral realm.*

While John-Roger never stopped discussing inner plane experiences, progressively less stress was placed on providing information about the lower planes as the Movement matured and as the astral projection fad faded away. Despite this slow shift in emphasis, J-R's basic approach and style has changed very little over the years. John-Roger has written dozens of books, conducted thousands of seminars, and provided material for hundreds of hours of taped lectures over the past several decades, but comparatively little has been added to the basic themes laid out in the first few years of his spiritual teaching activity. At the same time, J-R has said that as the Spirit moves him with greater clarity, he also moves with greater clarity; therefore, the teachings are constantly undergoing slight revisions, and, from the point of view of participants, the teachings go deeper and deeper with time.

In contrast to his simple, unadorned teaching style, another characteristic of John-Roger's activities has been a steady stream of usual psychic-spiritual experiences among his students. These experiences have characterized his ministry from the very beginning. Some sense of this dimension of J-R's activities has already been conveyed in the preceding story of the early days of MSIA. These experiences have come to be accepted as what we might call "everyday miracles" by many people in the Movement. Such experiences provide, as I indicated in the introduction, evidence for the reality of the subtle, inner levels that are not immediately accessible to our ordinary, everyday state of consciousness.

It is difficult to convey an accurate sense of the role these often remarkable events have played in the life of MSIA. From the perspective of MSIA's ultimate goal, Soul Transcendence, such experiences are insignificant. Not a few members, and even some who have been around for many years, have never had a single experience. For others, such psychic-spiritual experiences have been crucial for their personal spiritual journey. A remarkable example of this latter category of person is an actress whom I will call Susan Kelly (not her real name). In an interview I had with Kelly, she related a number of such experiences, including the story of how she feels John-Roger helped her land a big film role in the early days of her association with MSIA. In Kelly's words:

> *One night during a live seminar, we were supposed to send up a little memo to J-R, and you could ask him a question. So, I wrote, "Dear J-R, I would like to put in the Light with you, this role I really want in Bite the Bullet." When he got to the note, J-R looked right at me.*

"You've already gotten that role in the spirit. Don't show them the film Coming Apart. You were going to show them this film you did? You were in a different frequency when you did that film."

Well, you better believe it. I was on drugs. I was totally, stark raving nude. I was everything in that film. It was done in '68 and '69, before I got on the spiritual path.

"No need to show them that film. You already have the role." A couple of days later I got a call from Mr. Brooks' secretary that I'm supposed to show up on a Sunday. Would I mind showing up on a Sunday because he was doing these readings very quickly and had planned to costume everyone on Monday? So I said, "Sure."

The next day, I broke out with an infection that caused a rash all over my face. I'd been to Hawaii shooting "Hawaii 5-0," and I'd picked up something in Hawaii. It certainly wasn't sexual because I had been celibate, but it was just like staph all over me.

So I called up this guy who was the editor of The Movement newspaper at the time. His name was Joel.

"Joel, I gotta talk to John-Roger."

"Well, that's not easy, you know. You can't just say, 'I gotta talk to John-Roger.' He's a busy man; he's always traveling and teaching."

"You don't understand. He told me I was going to get this role, but now I've broken out in a staph infection. I've got to talk to him right away."

"Well, I want to give you this number at his personal residence, but you're not supposed to have it, Susan. So don't say where you got it from."

So I call this number, and he picks up the phone.

"Hi, Susan."

"I'd like to speak to John-Roger."

"This is John-Roger, Susan."

"Oh, well, I don't mean to disturb you, John-Roger, but I have this rash all over my face, and you told me I was going to get this role, blah-blah-blah-blah-blah."

"OK, look." He said, "[You're] probably very infectious now. If so, you shouldn't get near anyone. If I were you, I'd stay inside for three days, perhaps get a hold of some kelp, lecithin, and B-6, and chant and meditate around the clock. I'd also take kelp, lecithin, and B-6 like you can't get enough of it. If anyone brings you food, have them leave it at the door. I'm going to work with you on the other side and speak with your spirit guides on the other side."

Well, I didn't know what "speak with my spirit guides" meant, so I didn't know what was going on. But I said, "Fine, whatever."

Finally, he came back on and said, "Tuesday."

"What do you mean, 'Tuesday'? You're the Mystical Traveler. What's the matter with Sunday? My audition's Sunday." The minute I said it, I thought, "Man, I've got an ego!" I mean, I was hearing myself talk to this man that all these people were so devoted to, and I was making demands.

So while I was saying, "You're the Mystical Traveler; how come you're not going to get me well by Sunday?" he said, "Tuesday."

So he goes away and he puts Muzak on. Suddenly "The Impossible Dream" is playing on the phone, and I'm thinking, "Man, this is corny! This has gotta be the corniest thing I've ever heard. I'm listening to "The Impossible Dream" and he's talking to my spirit guides on the other side. What's going on?"

But he came back and he said, "O.K. After you hang up, just see if you can just go to bed and don't talk to anyone for a while. Do your spiritual exercises, and you'll be fine."

So the next day I'd done everything he said, and it was beginning to go away. Then it was getting close to Sunday, and it's not all gone, so I was getting a bit freaked out. I still had the scabs and whatnot, and it's like Friday and it's getting to be Saturday, and I'm like freaking. Suddenly I get a phone call. It was Mr. Brooks' secretary.

"Susan, would you mind if we switch you to Tuesday? Because Mr. Brooks has a sudden unexpected engagement."

"No! No! That will be just fine!"

Well, Tuesday came. My face was entirely clear. I had one little tiny bump down there. You couldn't see it unless you were looking for it. But, I was so used to a face filled with scabs that I was horrified someone was going to know.

So I got all dressed up and I went in there and he said, "Well, kid, we gotta make your hair brown, gotta have you have long hair. I want you to look like my wife, Jean Simmons. Going to get you fitted for a hair fall. Hair down to your waist, dark brown, whatnot."

"You mean, I get the part?"

"Yeah, you got the part, kid."

"Well, Mr. Brooks, don't pay any attention to this thing," I said, pointing to my bump.

"What are you talking about, kid?"

"This thing."

"Shut up, kid. You're going to lose the part if you don't shut up. Just go to costumes."

Then I went off on location with Gene Hackman and the rest of them.

While Kelly's story may strike the reader as outside the realm of ordinary human experience, such "everyday miracles" are not viewed as extraordinary events by MSIA veterans who have heard many such stories over the years and have experienced things like this themselves.

Reflecting the counterculture's interest in communal living arrangements as well as the model of the ashrams and monasteries being established by the new Asian spiritual groups, many early Movement participants felt that MSIA should establish a spiritual household. After a couple of initial experiments with different residences (e.g., a large house referred to as the "Light Castle" served this purpose for a few years), the Movement acquired an old mansion that, prior to their acquisition of the property, had been expanded and converted into a retirement home for doctors.

Purchased in 1974, this house in L.A.'s Crenshaw district was designated "Prana" (a Sanskrit word referring to the subtle energies tapped by certain yogic techniques). From then until now it has served as MSIA headquarters, though John-Roger never made it his residence. In the early days, over a hundred people lived in the Prana complex, and many other Movement participants resided in an adjoining apartment complex. Listening to the stories members tell of this period, one comes away with the impression that Prana served as a kind of spiritual "basic training" center for many young aspirants.

As the Movement and its members matured, the interest in communal living waned. The population of Prana eventually decreased from a high of about 130, to, at present, thirty-some-odd people, mostly core staff. The facility now serves as organizational headquarters and as a seminary — Peace

Theological Seminary and College of Philosophy (often referred to by the abbreviation "PTS") — and the bedrooms that formerly held avid ashramites have found new usefulness as dorm rooms for visiting students. PTS offers a variety of classes, correspondence courses, and a 2-year Master of Theology degree to Movement participants (the program has also been held outside of Los Angeles in other areas of the country), and there are plans to institute a course of study for a Doctor of Theology degree. As someone who has casually observed the Master of Theology program develop, my impression is that it has become one of the MSIA organization's core activities.

How the Movement spread beyond southern California to other parts of the country is another part of the MSIA story.

This juncture in the Movement's development is, however, quite complex because the story line splits off into separate narratives for each area. Rather than attempting to tell all of these tales, I will note a few points that will provide some perspective on the organization's expansion.

In the early days, the teachings were spread outside of California via people sending tape recordings of John-Roger seminars to relatives and friends in other parts of the country. These friends or relatives would then hold home seminars at which J-R tapes would be played. (This seems, in fact, to have been the actual origin of the "taped" as opposed to the "live" seminar.) At first these tapes were quite crude — people initially recorded John-Roger's talks with omni-directional microphones on cassette records — and the switch to more professionally-recorded sessions was prompted by complaints about tape quality from other areas of the country. One of the first MSIA "beachheads" outside of California was the Miami, Florida, area. During an interview, one longtime member related an amusing story about her first experience at a taped seminar in south Florida in 1969:

*I went to the address, and it was one of these tene-
ment apartment buildings with the exposed light
bulbs outside of each apartment. So I knocked on the
door. Someone opened it a little, and it was dark
inside. I said, "Is this where they play the tapes?" I
didn't even know anything more specific to ask. So he
said, "Yeah," and opened the door, and I walked in
and it was like going into a movie theater when the
lights are down and you can't see. . . .*

*As my eyes began to adjust, I noticed squiggly
strings of different lengths hanging from the ceiling. .
. . Kind of a nouveau art thing. The center of the floor
was bare, there was no furniture, and people were sitting along the edge, leaning up against the walls. The
only thing in the middle of the room was a tape
machine. Nobody said, "Well, sit over here" — not
anything! It was weird. So I looked around for a
place to sit and I noticed that there was this La-Z-
Boy® chair, and behind the back of it was a wall
space. So I climbed under the chair to sit down.*

*The tape began to play, and it was the most hor-
rendous sounding thing. It had all this background
noise, and you really had to listen hard to hear anything. So I was sitting there in this remarkable place,
and it was all the most amazing scene. As I listened
to this tape I could not understand, in a room full of
people I had not met and could barely see, sitting on
the floor, something began to happen inside of me.
The most bewildering statement was made inside of
me — by me to me — and that was, "I'm home."*

Soon afterwards, the south Florida seminars shifted to a
home with less of a countercultural ambiance. In Miami, as in
other parts of the country, J-R would be invited out from L.A.

to hold live seminars and other events after a large enough group of interested, regular people had formed. However, while the strength and size of groups of MSIA participants in other areas waxed and waned, MSIA never, as an organization, established formal centers outside of southern California.

The story and the pattern of MSIA's expansion outside of the United States is not unlike the Movement's expansion across the country, though there are a couple of prominent cases — Africa and Australia come to mind — where the initial contact came from individuals who had read a piece of MSIA literature and wrote for more information. In other cases, people who had studied with the Movement in the U.S. moved overseas and started holding home seminars in their country of residence.

As will be discussed in detail in Chapter Seven, over half of all currently active Movement participants reside in the United States. Of these, around 40% live in California. The impression of MSIA as still being centered in the Los Angeles basin is reinforced by the fact that, as a corporate entity, most properties owned by the Church are in southern California. In other parts of the country as well as overseas, Movement activity has been largely confined to home seminars, with occasional visits by J-R, John Morton, or some other person empowered to hold live seminars. One reason why MSIA has not established a larger presence outside of California is the tendency among participants from other parts of the country to move to the L.A. area in order to be closer to the Traveler and to the Movement's organizational center.

A different kind of organizational expansion arose from John-Roger's active experimentation with different vehicles for the teachings. While the basic ideas have remained the same over the years, there has been a remarkable proliferation of classes, spinoff organizations, and other activities since the Movement's beginnings. This diversification is a reflection of

John-Roger's open-ended, let's-try-this-and-see-if-it-works attitude.

A particularly important development for the Movement's expansion in the seventies was the adoption and modification of the then-popular est/Lifespring seminars. Russell Bishop had been a trainer for Lifespring, and he proposed to J-R that a Lifespring training be held specifically for Movement people. It was given at the Miramar Hotel in Santa Monica.

Anywhere from 100 to 200 people attended. One person remembers that this was "so popular that it led to many other trainings." John-Roger told me that, "Insight came later, after much reflection as to how Lifespring didn't really work for us and how we wanted to put the Spirit into it and, therefore, change many of the Lifespring processes to fit what Insight wanted to do."

One longtime member said it this way:

> *Insight kind of took the format of Lifespring and made it loving. There wasn't an "asshole theater" like there was in Lifespring, and there wasn't an in-your-face attitude. It was more loving.*
>
> *It was during one of the early trainings that I had one of those experiences that gave me a greater awareness of what we were doing, what was going on, what the Discourses were talking about, what J-R was talking about, etc. If my whole life goes by and I have the memory of that one experience, there's nothing that I can't face because of that experience. That can't be taken away. That can't be negated by the naysayers, or the people who have left that are basing their dislike of what we're doing on their physical realm experiences, because it was not a physical experience.*

Initially Insight was closely associated with MSIA, and a great many people in the Movement took Insight training. At present, Insight operates completely independently of John-Roger and MSIA, and, further, is not (and never was) regarded as an MSIA training.

The transformation of the Lifespring style into the more caring Insight style is typical of John-Roger's experimental attitude: Take something from somewhere else that works, and modify it until it becomes congruent with the MSIA approach.

Other organizations founded by John-Roger and/or MSIA members were Baraka Holistic Healing Center (1976) and the John-Roger Foundation (1982). The John-Roger Foundation was created in order to raise funds for nonprofit organizations and sponsor classes, seminars, and symposiums. Along with the Integrity Foundation (incorporated in 1983), the JRF celebrated Integrity Day, through which the Foundations could promote global transformation by the enrichment and upliftment of individuals. An annual Integrity Award banquet was held for five years beginning in 1983: During this event, awards were given to individuals for their achievement along with checks which were donated to their favorite charities. Among the recipients of the integrity awards were Dr. Jonas Salk, Bishop Desmond Tutu, Lech Walesa, and Mother Theresa.

In 1988, the John-Roger Foundation altered its focus, and changed its corporate name to the Foundation for the Study of Individual and World Peace. These organizations operate independently of MSIA. Even MSIA is set up to run independently of the advice and input of John-Roger, though as the founder and original teacher, his suggestions naturally exert tremendous influence.

As should be clear by this point, the Church of the Movement of Spiritual Inner Awareness and the other organizations that have been inspired by John-Roger and MSIA members are the products of a gradual process of growth. All of these structures were significantly shaped by J-R's input in their earliest stages. However, far from constituting a monolithic block, most of these have expanded out from underneath the umbrella of MSIA and matured beyond the need for the ongoing personal tutelage of John-Roger.

There was some point, and maybe there has been more than one point, where J-R said, "I basically have finished what I came here to do, what was my job, my responsibility, as the Traveler." And when he said it, he didn't keel over and die. Instead, he kept doing work and seminars. But I picked up that statement as, "Okay, the key information, whatever it was here for him to do, he did." The way I related to it was, it's been passed on, so that whatever I need to pick up about soul consciousness through the Traveler, has been delivered to me, it's been placed into my hands, the information is available, and the energy fields are on the planet.

—John Morton

3

MOVEMENT BACKGROUND AND SOME RELIGIOUS/PHILOSOPHICAL TRADITIONS PRECEDING MSIA

From a historical perspective, the Movement of Spiritual Inner Awareness can be understood as a synthesis of many different, preexisting practices and philosophies. The two principal components of this synthesis are India's 500-year-old Sant Mat tradition and the West's occult-metaphysical subculture — the subculture that gave birth to the New Age movement. As the successor movement to the counterculture of the 1960s, the New Age had become a significant subculture by the mid-1970s. This subculture proved fertile ground for the birth and growth of such new churches as the Movement of Spiritual Inner Awareness. As the matrix out of which MSIA emerged and from which the Movement continues to be nourished, the New Age subculture has profoundly shaped the face of MSIA.

In this chapter, I will present overviews of this subculture and the Sant Mat tradition, and then examine how MSIA is simultaneously related to — yet distinct from — both. As a way of working our way into this discussion, I want to relate an experience from a New Age (non-MSIA) retreat that will serve as a point of reference for some of the points I will be making later in the analysis.

The Occult/Metaphysical/"New Age" Subculture

In April of 1990, I flew to Maui to attend the Spring Renewal, a gathering at a YMCA camp on the northeast side of the island at which participants (mostly "New Agers" who live on the island) come together to renew their spiritual life. The basic idea behind such gatherings is not new — the same general notion informed the annual camp meetings that were part of nineteenth century Evangelical Protestantism — but in most other ways the activities that take place during Spring Renewal depart markedly from the camp meetings of the past century.

The workshop that had the most personal impact for me occurred early in the retreat. The workshop leader began with a discussion of women's repression across the ages and led into an analysis of the tension between the sexes that has been generated as a result of the oppressor-oppressed relationship. As part of this discussion, reference was made to the idyllic, primordial goddess religion that — in this New Age "fall-from-Eden" myth — was supposed to have been the original religion of humankind (before its suppression by males and male deities). The conventional academic in me winced at the dubious scholarship that lay behind this uncritically appropriated tenet of New Age thought. The presentation did not, however, dwell on this point, but rather went on to deal with other issues.

The charismatic teacher leading the workshop gradually worked his way from historical generalities to personal specificities, eventually asking us to reflect on how we had hurt, and been hurt by, the various romantic partners we had encountered over the years. Infrequent are the relationships that end on a note of compassion and mutual understanding; far more common are the broken relationships that leave us with deep feelings of resentment, guilt, or both. Such feelings linger as emotional burdens that keep us from fully opening up to each new experience of love. In an ideal world, he went on to say, we might be able to recontact all of our old lovers and try to effect a better resolution to our broken relationships. But, even if that were logistically possible, it would be unlikely that we would be able to completely heal all of the old bitterness. Such was the gist of the discussion that led up to a group exercise, an exercise I cannot describe with any hope of doing justice to the experience.

We stood up and formed two circles, one consisting of approximately forty males and the other of about the same number of females, and were instructed to successively ask each person of the opposite sex to forgive us and to accept our love. The exercise was quite structured: We held hands and said, "I ask your forgiveness." Our partners responded by saying, "I forgive you." We then said, "I offer you my love," and our partners responded with, "I accept your love." The men first requested forgiveness of all of the women, and then the women requested forgiveness of all of the men. While we went through this exchange, we were asked to try to see the other person as someone of the opposite sex we needed to forgive (relatives as well as ex-lovers), or as someone by whom we wanted to be forgiven. As we were forming the circles, I knew that the exercise would be powerful, but I was not prepared for the intensity of the actual experience. Had I had a clearer inkling of what was about to occur, I probably would have run away (or, at least, have excused myself for a restroom break and not returned for a couple of hours).

To the extent that it is possible, I ask the reader to imaginatively place himself or herself in my situation: I tried to bring as much sincerity to each person as I could muster, although at first I had to at least partially "act out" the exercise. It was not long, however, before the experience became quite intense. After looking into the eyes of only a few women — people who really seemed to be offering me complete forgiveness — I began to drop my protective barriers and open up to the experience. I very quickly found myself genuinely asking for forgiveness for the many times I had consciously or unconsciously hurt my romantic partners. I do not remember at what point I began weeping, but I do remember that when I reached the camp yoga instructor I let go of the last shreds of my resistance. The instructor herself was red-faced from crying, and the fullness of her sincerity allowed me to feel completely forgiven. A lifetime of pain and guilt washed through me, followed by a wave of forgiveness and love. I felt reborn. The reciprocal experience seemed less difficult. Perhaps it was because I already felt open, or because I had already been forgiven by every female in the room, or some combination of these. But at that point I was ready to forgive all of womankind for every offense, real or imagined, that its members had ever committed against me.

The initial comparison I made with the Christian tradition was the parallel between Spring Renewal and the camp meetings of American Protestantism: As I noted, the idea of gathering together to renew one's spiritual life is basic to both. There is, however, a deeper parallel between New Age spirituality and Christian spirituality, a parallel that had escaped me until it was forcibly brought to my attention during this workshop. The parallel is that both hold out the promise of forgiveness.

No matter how hard we work on becoming better people, whether we are Christians, New Agers, or Secular Humanists, we often feel burdened by our past mistakes and misdeeds — by our sins, if you will. This "knot" of incompletely resolved issues from the past, which we can never fully undo by isolated acts of expiation, weighs us down and prevents us from growing into that New Being that we look to as our highest potential. The "good news" that both traditional Christianity and the New Age extend to the weary traveler is that forgiveness is possible, and that all one really has to do is to accept it — but, and here is the problem, accepting forgiveness turns out to be difficult, far more difficult than it at first appears.

What I did not know (or was not fully aware of) before my Maui experience, but which any traditional revival preacher could probably have told me, was that it is hard to accept being forgiven. We cannot forgive ourselves because we do not feel that we deserve forgiveness, so how can we ever be pardoned? This paradox keeps true "redemption" — true "forgiveness of sins" — from ever being a simple matter and is why traditional conversion accounts sometimes appear to be exaggerated exercises in self-analysis and self-torment.

When I later took my personal experience of New Age "redemption" as a lens through which to view the Movement more generally, I found myself becoming less critical of the New Age emphasis on the self. While admonitions to "love yourself," "forgive yourself," et cetera can, of course, be taken to narcissistic extremes, there is a more profound dimension to such discourse about the self than I was previously willing to acknowledge. Once we feel that we are forgiven, we are empowered to act in new and potentially healing ways, such as being able to genuinely forgive others. John-Roger goes so far as to portray the process of forgiveness as a portal to enlightened consciousness:

> As you gain wisdom, you go into forgiveness. You forgive yourself your own stupidity and ignorance and lack of knowledge, and you forgive everybody

else in the same instant. And at that moment, you're moving into enlightenment.

I have chosen to focus on the meaning of one event. I could, however, have related other realizations no less profound that I have experienced while doing fieldwork at other New Age gatherings. These encounters were a far cry from the commercialized spirituality that the mass media has chosen to portray as being at the heart of this movement. What was most evident to me during the Spring Renewal were people seeking a deeper understanding of themselves and of the larger universe of which we are a part. While I was far from being an uncritical participant, and while the people I met were far from perfect, I came away impressed by the event as well as by the intelligence, sincerity, and mutual caring of the other participants. During the time I spent on Maui, the more superficial, sensationalistic side of the New Age movement felt very far away indeed.

This is not, of course, to deny that the less-inspiring side exists. But judging the Movement solely on the merits of its least reputable aspects — such as some of the silly, grandiose claims made during even sillier channeling sessions — would be comparable to judging Christianity on the merits of televangelists like Jim and Tammy Bakker. Few people would be willing to condemn all of Christianity on the basis of its least-exemplary side, and the New Age should be approached with a similar evenhandedness.

If, however, the New Age movement is more than just a flaky survival of the hippie counterculture, what is it? The New Age can be viewed as a revivalist movement within a pre-existing metaphysical-occult community. As such, the New Age can be compared with Christian revivals, particularly with such phenomena as the early Pentecostal movement (a movement that simultaneously revived and altered a segment of Protestant Christianity). Comparable to the influence of Pentecostalism on Christianity, the New Age had an impact on some but not all segments of the occult community. Also like Pentecostalism, the New Age revival left a host of new organizations/denominations in its wake.

From another angle, the New Age can be viewed as a successor movement to the counterculture of the 1960s. As observers of the New Age have pointed out, a significant portion of New Agers are baby boomers, people who two decades earlier were probably participating, at some level, in the phenomenon known as the counterculture, if only at the level of fashion and popular music. As the counterculture faded away in the early seventies, many former "hippies" found themselves embarking on a spiritual quest — one that, in many cases, departed from the Judeo-Christian mainstream. Thus, one of the possible ways to date the beginnings of the New Age movement is from the period of the rather sudden appearance of large numbers of unconventional spiritual seekers in the decade following the sixties.

Narrowly considered as a social movement held together by specific ideas, the New Age can be traced to England in the late 1950s. At that time, the leaders of certain independent occult groups heavily influenced by the reading of theosophical authors, especially Alice Bailey, began to meet to discuss the possible changes coming during the last quarter of the twentieth century. Those meetings continued through the 1960s and, as they grew, came to include their most well-known participants — the founders of the Findhorn Community in Scotland. By the 1970s, a vision of the New Age had been clarified, and the movement was ready to reach out to like-minded people around the globe. The process of spreading was greatly assisted by the work of Anthony Brooke and the Universal Foundation. Brooke toured the world, contacting occult and metaphysical groups, and created the first international networks of New Age believers. David Spangler, a student of the Alice Bailey writings, traveled to England in 1970 and stayed at Findhorn for three years. Upon his return to the United States, he began to author a series of books, which laid out the hopes and aspirations of the New Age.

One can pinpoint certain essential ideas which came to distinguish the New Age movement. None are particularly new ideas, their distinctiveness being in their being brought together in a new gestalt:

> 1. *The possibility of personal transformation.* The New Age movement offers the possibility of a personal transformation in the immediate future. While personal transformation is a common offering of some occult and New Thought groups, it is usually presented as the end result of a long-term process of alteration through extensive training in the occult life (in conscious contrast to the immediate transformation offered by revivalist Christianity). Thus, the New Age, without radically changing traditional occultism, offered a new immediacy which had been lacking in metaphysical teachings.
>
> The transformative process is most clearly seen in the healing process, and transformation often is first encountered as a healing of the individual, either of a chronic physical problem or of a significant psychological problem. Healing has become a metaphor of transformation with the New Age movement. The stress on transformation and healing (in the sense of healing blocks to soul awareness) is clearly evident in MSIA's teachings.

2. *The coming of broad cultural transformation.* The
New Age movement offered the hope that the world,
which many people, especially those on the edges of
the dominant culture, experience in negative terms,
would in the next generation be swept aside and
replaced with a golden era. As articulated by spokes-
people like David Spangler, the hoped for changes are
placed in a sophisticated framework of gradual
change relying upon human acceptance of the new
resources and their creating a new culture. According
to Spangler, a watershed in human history has been
reached with the advent of modern technology and
its possibilities for good and evil. At the same time,
because of unique changes in the spiritual world,
symbolized and heralded (but not caused) by the
astrological change into the Aquarian Age, this generation has a unique bonus of spiritual power available to it. It is this additional spiritual energy operating on the world and its peoples that makes possible
the personal and cultural transformation that will
bring in a New Age.

It is, of course, the millennial hope of the coming
of a Golden Age of peace and light that gave the New
Age movement its name. This millennialism also provided a basis for a social consciousness that has been
notably lacking in most occult metaphysics. Once
articulated, the New Age vision could be and was
grounded in various endeavors designed to assist the
transition to the New Age. The New Age movement
wedded itself to environmentalism, lay peace movements, animal rights, women's rights, and cooperative forms of social organization.

On the theme of millennial transformation, MSIA departs significantly from the New Age. While many Church members are clearly working to improve society, MSIA as an organization is focused on Soul Transcendence rather than on world transformation.

3. *The transformation of occult arts and processes.* Within the New Age movement one finds all of the familiar occult practices from astrology to tarot, from mediumship to psychic healing. Yet in the New Age movement the significance of these practices has been significantly altered. Astrology and tarot are no longer fortune-telling devices, but have become tools utilized for self-transformation. Mediumship has become channeling, in which the primary role of the medium is to expound metaphysical truth, rather than to prove the continuance of life after death. Spiritual healing launches and undergirds a healing relationship to life.

The number of practitioners of astrology, tarot, mediumship, and psychic healing had been growing steadily throughout the twentieth century. Thus the New Age movement did not have to create its own professionals *de novo*, rather it had merely to transform and bring into visibility the large army of practitioners of the occult arts already in existence.

Possibly the most widely practiced New Age transformative tool is meditation (in its many varied forms) and related tools of inner development. In its utilization of meditation, the New Age movement borrowed insights from the findings of the human potential movement and transpersonal psychology, both of which, in isolating various practices for study, demonstrated that techniques of meditation and inner development could be detached from the religious teachings in which they were traditionally embedded. Thus, one could practice Zen meditation without being a Buddhist and yoga without being a Hindu. That insight made all of the Eastern, occult, and metaphysical techniques immediately available to everyone without the necessity of their changing self-identifying labels prior to their use. MSIA generally aligns with the New Age reinterpretation of meditative techniques, though the organization has not made the other occult arts part of its teachings, and specifically cautions against giving up responsibility for making one's own decisions by going to psychics, fortune-tellers, "readers," or anyone outside of oneself.

4. *The self as divine.* Within the New Age, one theological affirmation that has found popular support is the identification of the individual with the divine. Underlying this notion, which finds a wide variety of forms, is a monistic world in which the only reality is "God," usually thought of in predominantly impersonal terms as *mind* or *energy*. This is a tenet the New Age shares with traditional Upanishadic Hinduism (discussed below). Again, MSIA is clearly in synch with this dominant idea of New Age thinking, although its teachings simultaneously posit the alternative possibility of a personal, loving relationship with God.

Thus the New Age movement, narrowly defined, can be seen as an occult-metaphysical revival movement generated among independent British theosophists in the post-World

War II generation, which spread through the well-established occult-metaphysical community in the 1970s. Through the 1980s it became a popular movement, which enlivened the older occult-metaphysical community and which both drew many new adherents to it and greatly assisted the spread of occult practices (such as astrology and meditation) and ideas (such as reincarnation) into the general population far beyond the boundaries of the New Age movement proper.

The New Age is a synthesis of many different preexisting movements and strands of thought. In the early 1970s, the movement was characterized by the prominence of newly imported Asian groups, although many of the older occult-metaphysical organizations were also experiencing a growth spurt. These various groups, in combination with a significant number of less formally affiliated individuals, constituted a fairly substantial spiritual subculture that became the successor movement to the counterculture. This initial phase of the New Age movement looked forward to the transformation of society, but did not place an emphasis on many of the things that outside observers now regard as quintessentially New Age.

Emerging in the 1970s, MSIA was fully formed as a mature organization before phenomena such as channeling and crystals became faddish within New Age circles, and these did not become incorporated into the MSIA synthesis. However, some of the earlier New Age healing techniques dealing with different aspects of the self were adopted by MSIA, such as "aura balancing," "innerphasings," and "polarity balancing." (These techniques will be described in the next chapter.)

At this point, the reader may well be asking himself or herself, What does the proliferation of an alternative religious subculture mean for society as whole? There have been a variety of historical periods during which religious innovation flourished. In the West, there was a proliferation of a new

religious consciousness in the late classical period, as well as in
the wake of the Reformation. In the United States, historians
have noted a recurring pattern of religious awakenings, beginning with the Great Awakening of the 1740s.

The most general observation we can make is that periods
of renewed spiritual activity occur in the wake of disruptive
social and economic changes: The established vision of "how
things work" no longer seems to apply, and people begin
searching for new visions. In previous cycles of American religious experimentation, innovative forms of Protestantism
often formed the basis for these new visions. As revivalist fer-
vor died down, new or reinvigorated Protestant denominations became the pillars of a new cultural hegemony. The most
recent period of American religious innovation occurred in the
decades following the demise of the 1960s counterculture.
However, unlike previous cycles of revival, the religious explo-
sion that occurred in the 1970s and 1980s has not provided a
basis for a new spiritual and cultural synthesis. While there has
been a growth in conservative Protestant denominations during this period (a growth parallel to the pattern of earlier
Awakenings), there has also been a marked growth in "metaphysical" religion. The most visible manifestation of this latter
strand of spirituality has been the New Age movement, which
offers a vision of the world fundamentally different from that
of traditional Christianity. Thus, during this most recent cycle
of religious enthusiasm, Protestantism has failed to reestablish
its traditional hegemony over American culture.

South Asia and the Sant Mat Tradition

Beyond the considerable influence of the New Age, the other
major component of MSIA is South Asian religiosity, particularly as South Asian religion is embodied in the Sant Mat tradition. Hinduism is the blanket term for the indigenous reli-

gious tradition of the South Asian (Indian) subcontinent. It is constituted by a broad diversity of beliefs and practices that, at their extremes, bear little resemblance to one another. Hinduism's sometimes mind-boggling diversity is at least partially a result of the complex history of the Indian subcontinent, which, over the millennia, has seen innumerable influxes of different peoples from outside South Asia. Around 1,500–1,000 B.C.E. or much earlier, according to Hindu scholars, a group of aggressive pastoral peoples from central Asia invaded India through the northern mountain passes and conquered the indigenous people. These peoples, who called themselves Aryans ("Nobles"), originated from around the Caspian Sea.

The worldview of the Aryan invaders of India was preserved in a group of (originally oral) texts, the *Vedas*. After settling down in the Indian subcontinent, the Aryans became more introspective, started asking questions about the ultimate meaning of life, and developed an ideology centered around release or liberation (*moksha*) from the cycle of death and rebirth (*samsara*). The various disciplines that are collectively referred to as yoga developed out of this introspective turn.

A group of religious texts called the *Upanishads* postulated an eternal, changeless core of the self that was referred to as the Atman. This soul or deep self was viewed as being identical with the unchanging godhead, referred to as Brahman (the unitary ground of being that transcends particular gods and goddesses). The equating of the deep self with the ultimate is expressed in innumerable ways, such as in the Upanishadic formula *Tat tvam asi* ("Thou art that!"), meaning that the essential "you" is the same as that indescribable ("Where from words turn back") essence of everything:

> *He who, dwelling in all things, yet is other than all things, whom all things do not know, whose body all*

*things are, who controls all things from within — He
is your soul, the Controller, the Immortal.*

Untouched by the variations of time and circumstance, the Atman was nevertheless entrapped in the world of *samsara*. Samsara is the South Asian term for the world we experience in our everyday lives. This constantly changing, unstable world is contrasted with the spiritual realm of Atman/Brahman, which by contrast is stable and unchanging. Samsara also refers to the process of death and rebirth (reincarnation) through which we are "trapped" in this world. Unlike many Western treatments of reincarnation, which make the idea of coming back into body after body seem exotic, desirable, and even romantic, Hinduism, Buddhism, and other South Asian religions portray the samsaric process as unhappy: Life in this world is suffering.

What keeps us trapped in the samsaric cycle is the law of karma. In its simplest form, this law operates impersonally like a natural law, ensuring that every good or bad deed eventually returns to the individual in the form of reward or punishment commensurate with the original deed. It is the necessity of "reaping one's karma" that compels human beings to take rebirth (to reincarnate) in successive lifetimes. In other words, if one dies before reaping the effects of one's actions (as most people do), the karmic process demands that one return in a future life. Coming back into another lifetime also allows karmic forces to reward or punish one through the circumstance in which one is born. Hence, for example, an individual who was generous in one lifetime might be reborn as a wealthy person in his or her next incarnation.

Moksha is the traditional Sanskrit term for release or liberation from the endless chain of deaths and rebirths. In the South Asian religious tradition, it represents the supreme goal of human strivings. Reflecting the diversity of Hinduism, liberation can be attained in a variety of different ways, from the proper performance of certain rituals to highly disciplined forms of yoga. In the *Upanishads*, it is proper knowledge, in the sense of insight into the nature of reality, that enables the aspiring seeker to achieve liberation from the wheel of rebirth.

What happens to the individual after reaching moksha? In Upanishadic Hinduism, the individual Atman is conceived of as merging into the cosmic Brahman. A traditional image is that of a drop of water, which, when dropped into the ocean, loses its individuality and becomes one with the ocean. While this metaphor is widespread, it does not quite capture the significance of this "merger." Rather than losing one's individuality, the Upanishadic understanding is that the Atman is never separate from Brahman; hence, individuality is illusory, and liberation is simply waking up from the dream of separateness.

The most that the classical texts of Hinduism say about the state of one who has merged with the godhead is that he or she has become one with pure "beingness," consciousness, and bliss.

In the wake of a series of devotional movements that swept across the subcontinent, various strands of "sectarianism" developed, focused on the worship of Vishnu/Krishna, Shiva, Durga/Kali, or some other form of the divine. The deity of one's sect was portrayed as the supreme god or goddess, and the other divinities envisioned as demigods or demigoddesses, inferior to the supreme. This high god/goddess was also seen as being the creator, a creator concerned with his or her creation and particularly concerned with the fate of human beings.

Despite these modifications, the samsaric cycle of death and rebirth was still viewed as unattractive, and the goal was still to achieve release from the cycle. By the time of Buddha (approximately 600 B.C.E.), the Indian consensus was that it was desire (passion, attachment, want, craving) that kept one involved in the karmic process, and hence desire that kept one bound to the death/rebirth process. Consequently, the goal of getting off the Ferris wheel of reincarnation necessarily involved freeing oneself from desire.

To reduce the possibility of karma-producing actions, the Upanishadic tradition had tended to view asceticism/monasticism as the mode of life best suited to achieving the goal of release from samsara. However, by the time of the Bhagavad Gita, the earliest important work of devotional theism, another possibility had been thought through. Because it was the craving associated with activity that set the karmic process in motion, rather than the activity itself, the author (or authors) of the Bhagavad Gita developed the alternative approach of remaining in the everyday world while performing one's deeds with an attitude of dispassionate detachment. In the Gita, this detachment is discussed in terms of detachment from the "fruits of actions," meaning that actions are not undertaken for personal gain. Difficult though this may be, Krishna, who in the Gita is the principal spokesperson for this point of view, asserts that such a frame of mind is indeed possible if the individual will constantly maintain an attitude of devotion to God. When successful, one can even engage in such activities as war (as long as one is fighting because it is one's duty) and avoid the negative karma that would normally result from such actions.

During the devotional revivals that swept across South Asia during the Indian middle ages, a strand of spirituality developed in Northwest India that came to be referred to as the Sant Mat tradition. Like other devotional paths, this new tradition was built around devotion to a single divinity. However, unlike the others, Sant Mat portrayed the divine as an essentially formless God who, unlike Krishna, Shiva, and so forth, did not enter into incarnation on the earth. Instead, he was represented by a guru who taught one how to reconnect with the divine source. MSIA's core spiritual practices lie in the Sant tradition. Beyond these core practices, however, MSIA diverges significantly from Sant Mat. In an interview conducted toward the end of the present study, John-Roger stated that MSIA is neither a Sant Mat group, nor a Sant Mat-like group. MSIA is, rather, more like a simile of Sant Mat.

> *It's too much NOT like Sant Mat, because when you get further into MSIA teachings, you start to hear things about the basic self, and you get to hear things about such things as obsessions and possessions. You don't hear things like that in Sant Mat groups. You hear, "Worship the guru and he will lead you to salvation." In MSIA you hear, ". . . disregard who's bringing the message."*

Unlike Sant Mat, MSIA does not, for example, practice dietary restrictions, and members generally regard themselves as followers of the Christ Consciousness. In common with the religious traditions that have originated on the South Asian subcontinent, MSIA accepts the notion that the individual soul is caught up in the material world, which, though viewed less negatively than in classical Hinduism, is nevertheless less desirable than the state of liberation from this realm. However, like other religions in the South Asian tradition, MSIA members aim ultimately to be liberated from the cycle of death and rebirth.

In common with other Sant Mat groups, MSIA pictures the cosmos as composed of many different levels or "planes." At the point of creation, these levels sequentially emerged from God along a vibratory "stream" until creation reached its terminus in the physical plane. The Sant Mat tradition teaches that individuals can be linked to God's creative energy, and that this stream of energy will carry their consciousness back

to God. Although there are theological differences and some
minor technical variances in the different Sant organizations,
the basic tenets are shared by all groups.

Central to the teachings of the Sant Mat tradition is the
necessity of a living human master who is competent in initiating disciples into the practice and technique of listening to
the inner sound and contemplating the inner light (Surat
Shabd Yoga, referred to as "spiritual exercises" in MSIA).
While the Sant tradition refers to the living human master with
such honorifics as "guru," "Satguru," "Perfect Master," and
so forth, in MSIA the teacher is referred to as the Mystical
Traveler. The Mystical Traveler Consciousness is, however, a
somewhat different notion from that of "guru."

According to MSIA, each individual on the planet is
involved in his or her own movement of spiritual inner awareness, of which the Movement of Spiritual Inner Awareness is
an outward reflection. Individuals who wish to develop total
awareness and free themselves from the necessity of reincarnation can seek the assistance of the Mystical Traveler, who
holds the spiritual keys to Soul Transcendence and can assist
students in their quest. MSIA is devoted solely to supporting
people who are reaching toward Soul Transcendence.
However, the organization of MSIA is not necessary to the
spiritual work of the Mystical Traveler, which is seen as a consciousness existing on the planet from the very beginning
of time.

For example, MSIA holds that Jesus was a Mystical
Traveler. In this regard, John-Roger has even asserted that
Jesus Christ is ultimately the head of MSIA and is his (J-R's)
spiritual master. Furthermore, Jesus in his (present) ascended
state both embodies the Mystical Traveler Consciousness and
holds the office of Christ, as that office is understood in the
theosophical tradition (roughly analogous to a "presidency"
of the planet).

The Mystical Traveler, in the sense of a living person, has a complex relationship with the Mystical Traveler Consciousness (MTC), which is a much larger reality, and much harder to explain. The MTC is a bit like the Christian notion of the Holy Spirit, in the sense that the MTC is an impersonal yet conscious "energy" or "spirit" that seeks to spiritually uplift human beings. The Traveler Consciousness is also said to exist within each person on the planet, though some are more aware of this than others. The human being through whom the energy of the MTC flows is said to "anchor" the MTC into the physical realm — the world of our ordinary, everyday experience. Anchoring the energy allows it to become available for everyone to use for his or her spiritual upliftment. Thus, the MTC is described as being like a conveyer system or an "escalator" into the higher realms of Spirit.

The Mystical Traveler Consciousness is simultaneously aware of God as the formless Ground of Being and individualized souls and all of the evolving forms and environments of creation. As such, the MTC represents or mediates (or "mystically travels") between God and the souls and creation as an aspect of God that furthers cosmic evolution — a universal, compassionate intelligence that teaches, heals, uplifts, and liberates.

John-Roger formerly served as the anchor for the MTC, but in 1988 passed that function on to John Morton. In their roles as Mystical Travelers, John-Roger and John Morton are simultaneously greater and lesser than gurus — greater in the sense that the Mystical Traveler Consciousness is a larger notion than that of guruship; lesser in the sense that the person who "anchors" the MTC is an ordinary human being who is not identical with the MTC. Because it is the MTC that is the significant reality, MSIA initiates need not have a personal relationship with John-Roger or John Morton in order to follow the MSIA "path."

4

THE TEACHINGS: A LITTLE SOUL TRAVEL GOES A LONG WAY

You don't have to understand something that is already within you; you just have to awaken. . . .
—John-Roger

In Edwin Abbott's celebrated classic, *Flatland*, we are introduced to a square who is living a rather humdrum life as a lawyer in his native two-dimensional world. At the beginning of Flatland's third millennium, a sphere (whom the Square can perceive only as a circle) from Spaceland reveals the existence of the third dimension to the incredulous lawyer. The Sphere makes a number of efforts to explain the nature of three-dimensional space, but the Square, whose experience has always been confined to two dimensions, cannot even begin to imagine it.

After a rather lengthy and fruitless discussion with the Sphere, the Square finally concludes that the Sphere is insane and attempts to apprehend the Sphere by pinning him to the wall of his home with one of his (the Square's) corners. Jolted into action, the Sphere responds by moving upwards, thereby lifting the Square — who is pinned to his side — out of his two-dimensional world. The Sphere then forces the Square to see Flatland from the perspective of the third dimension. In the words of the fictional protagonist:

> *An unspeakable horror seized me. There was a dark-ness; then a dizzy, sickening sensation of sight that was not like seeing; I saw a Line that was no Line; Space that was not Space: I was myself and not myself. When I could find my voice, I shrieked aloud in agony, "Either this is madness or it is Hell!" "It is neither," calmly replied the voice of the Sphere, "it is Knowledge; it is Three Dimensions: open your eyes once again and try to look steadily." I looked, and behold, a new world!*

Abbott's story is, among other things, an allegory for the common human weakness of being blind to viewpoints other than our own. From a somewhat different perspective, *Flatland* is a useful metaphor for some of the self-imposed limitations of modernity.

The single most influential factor that has shaped the worldview of the modern mind is science. However, critics of modernity have frequently asserted that the contemporary, secular view of the world has been built on a misreading of science. This misreading is the not uncommon interpretation — often referred to as "scientism" — that the aspect of the world studied by the natural sciences is real while all other aspects are unreal. Thus, from the perspective of scientism, the real world is hard, cold, colorless, and silent; a world of dead matter in motion best apprehended in mathematical formulas. In this vision of reality, human beings and human consciousness are simply fortuitous accidents — incidental by-products of the workings of the machine of nature. In the context of this worldview, the only source of warmth is human relationships — relationships that are ultimately little more than a huddling together against the chill of a silent universe.

But is this viewpoint, more religiously inclined individuals might ask, really as universally obvious as its advocates maintain? Or is it only self-evident when we view the world through the framework of a rather narrow interpretation of natural science? Perhaps, to paraphrase an often-cited passage from William James, there exist alternative frames of reference, separated from us by the "filmiest of screens."

The basic idea of one or more "spiritual" worlds existing alongside the world of our ordinary, everyday experience in what we might call a different "dimension" is taken for granted in almost every religious and cultural tradition outside of the modern West. For many of these traditions, the spiritual realm is more important, and often more real, than the physical realm. Cross-culturally and across many different historical periods, there is widespread agreement on this point. An image often used to describe the process of becoming aware of this otherworld is the metaphor of awakening.

Call to mind a particularly vivid dream experience. In the midst of sleep, dreams are experienced as "real" rather than as "just a dream." As early as the fourth century B.C.E., Chuang-tzu, a Chinese philosopher, raised a series of profound and perplexing questions about dreams:

> *While men are dreaming, they do not perceive that it is a dream. Some will even have a dream in a dream, and only when they awake do they know it was all a dream. And so, when the Great Awakening comes upon us, shall we know this life to be a great dream. Fools believe themselves to be awake now.*

> *Once upon a time, I, Chuang-tzu, dreamed I was a butterfly, fluttering hither and thither, to all intents and purposes a butterfly. I was conscious only of following my fancies as a butterfly, and was unconscious of my individuality as a butterfly. Suddenly I was awakened, and there I lay myself again. Now I do not know whether I was a man dreaming I was a butterfly, or whether I am a butterfly now dreaming I am a man.*

In this passage, Chuang-tzu raises issues to which there can be several responses. In some traditional cultures, it is not unusual to place the reality of the realm of dreams on an equal footing with the realm of everyday consciousness, as Chuang-tzu appears to do in the above passage. Another line of reflection implicit in Chuang-tzu's remarks is the notion that perhaps the world as we ordinarily experience it is no more real than a dream.

In traditional Eastern philosophies the assertion that this world is, like a dream, illusory is commonplace. India outstrips other cultural traditions in the development of the theme of this life and/or this world as a kind of dream. Especially in the philosophical tradition of Advaita Vedanta, this metaphor is employed so as to stress the dreamlike quality — and hence the unreality — of the world as we experience it in our normal state of consciousness. The ultimate goal of the spiritual life, enlightenment or liberation, is often described as an awakening from the dream that deludes us into regarding the world of our everyday experience as real and important. These traditions are thus asking us to consider the possibility of a new kind of expanded awareness — states of consciousness so elevated they make our ordinary, everyday mental states appear dreamlike by comparison.

MSIA's understanding of the nature of reality is rooted in a traditional world view that perceives the physical world of our everyday experience to be but one facet — the lowest "story," so to speak — of a multidimensional cosmos. Within this worldview, the universe is understood to be intrinsically purposeful, and human life ultimately meaningful. The notion of a multi-layered reality is not unique to the Movement of Spiritual Inner Awareness. Although differing in many details, this view of the cosmos as a hierarchy of different levels of being was basic to virtually all known societies, thus constituting what philosopher Huston Smith has ventured to call "the human unanimity."

Various metaphors that this vision of reality call to mind are a ladder (e.g., Jacob's Ladder), a many-storied building, or a terraced hillside. This ladder-like image serves traditional worldviews in a manner comparable with the role performed by the image of ocean waves for the wave theory of light: It is a pictorial analogy that clarifies the theory by translating it into an image familiar to our sensory experience.

As with a scientific paradigm, problems can be created by interpreting a metaphysical model too literally. In some more archaic notions of other realms, for example, higher levels of reality were actually thought of as being located in the sky. More sophisticated notions of other realms are based on the spiritual experiences one has during meditation and during certain mystical states.

During meditation (referred to in MSIA as spiritual exercises, though MSIA teaches that its spiritual exercises are somewhat different from what is normally called meditation), one experiences an alteration of awareness that can be expressed, and which frequently is expressed, as an elevation of consciousness. Because these states of awareness vary in intensity or "elevation," the model of a hierarchy of levels is a useful conceptual tool for picturing these states of consciousness in relation to each other. This psychological model becomes a metaphysical paradigm by postulating that each state of consciousness corresponds with a different plane or level of being. It would be analogous to saying that during our dreams we leave one realm and enter another realm. It should be fairly easy to see both the usefulness of a ladder-like model in this context, and the nonliteral meaning of rising or sinking in consciousness.

Rather than literally being above or below, the other levels are conceptualized as coexisting with the physical plane, being separated from the physical by what some traditions refer to as a different "rate of vibration." These various levels remain distinct from each other in much the same way that different radio waves coexist in the same space without interfering with each other.

Correspondingly, the human self can be viewed as a series of concentric circles. The soul, which is the deepest and most real part of the individual, is situated at the center, metaphorically speaking, of a series of bodies or sheaths that correspond with the various levels of being. Although the source of consciousness is rooted in the soul level, it is normally focused outwards, away from the soul, and into one or more of the outer sheaths/lower bodies. In terms of this model, the goal of the spiritual life is to turn one's attention away from the outer layers and lead it back to the soul.

As explained in the preceding chapter, the Sant Mat tradition views these various levels as being linked by their vibrations — vibrations that together constitute the Sound Current. By connecting to the Sound Current through MSIA spiritual exercises, the individual places himself/herself on a roadway that leads back up through the various planes to the soul level. MSIA also teaches that there are realms beyond the soul level and that a person can transcend the initial level of soul and move in consciousness into these even higher levels. This, in essence, is what John-Roger means when he states that the goal of the Movement of Spiritual Inner Awareness is Soul Transcendence.

Intermediate between the physical realm and the soul realm are four planes, giving one a schema of six levels. In MSIA, these six realms are designated as follows:

soul	relating to who one essentially is
etheric	relating to the unconscious, in the sense that it is the gateway to the higher levels
mental	relating to the mind
causal	relating to the emotions
astral	relating to the imagination
physical	relating to our everyday lives

This terminology can be rather confusing to people who have studied other systems, such as theosophy or yoga. In these alternate traditions, the order of the planes is usually quite different, according to the following schema:

soul, causal, mental, astral, etheric, physical

As someone more than a little familiar with these other traditions, it took some effort for this writer to adjust to MSIA's terminology.

Terminology aside, however, the basic idea is essentially the same. Each level, from the physical to the soul, is increasingly refined or "subtle." Yet another analogy that suggests itself here is a comparison with different states of matter: The molecules in a solid object, such as a block of ice, can vibrate at different rates (i.e., different temperatures) without the object's losing its nature as a solid substance. However, if the molecules begin to vibrate fast enough, the solid changes into a liquid. In the case of H_2O, the block of ice will eventually be transformed into a puddle of water. Water, again, can vary considerably in temperature and remain a liquid. However, at the boiling point of water, it transforms once again, this time into gas. Similarly, the fundamental substance of which the various planes are composed is basically the same in essence. However, at the increasingly rarefied vibration of higher levels of being, this material becomes increasingly subtle, becoming completely different in appearance.

The world we bring into our awareness through the five senses, meaning the world we ordinarily experience in our everyday lives, is the *physical world*. As the level farthest from God or Spirit, the physical realm is insubstantial, like the shadows in Plato's *Allegory of the Cave*. It is also a realm of delusion that can easily distort our higher vision, enabling us, in John-Roger's words, to "perpetrate against ourselves the belief that no other levels exist because we cannot see them."

In MSIA's schema, the next realm up is the *astral level*. The astral is the world of the imagination (the "image-making" aspect of the mind), and it is the level at which most dreams occur. As the realm of the imagination, the "substance" of the astral world is amenable to the power of the human mind, enabling one to create "structures" out of astral substance. Because of its responsiveness to the imagination, the higher parts of the astral are very beautiful, creating a heavenlike world in which many departed individuals reside. In contrast, the lower astral is responsive to our fears and bad thoughts, creating a realm of negativity that we sometimes tap into in our nightmares.

The next level up is the *causal*, which is the cause and effect realm of the emotions. MSIA teaches that this is the realm in which we work out most of our emotional turmoil. While most people dream at the astral level, the dreaming consciousness sometimes travels to higher realms, particularly when the dreamer is treading the spiritual path. When we dream at the causal level, we awaken with a strong emotion — loving the whole world or hating the whole world — but recalling few dream images.

The *mental world* is the realm of the universal mind. John-Roger teaches that most of the geniuses of the planet have come from this realm, and that New Thought religions like Unity and Science of Mind draw their energy from the mental level. When we dream at this level, we awaken with the sense that we were taught something during the night. We may recall being in a class, hearing a lecture, or reading a book.

The *etheric world* is hard to describe. The best we can do with ordinary language is to say that it is a transitional realm between the soul and the lower worlds. In John-Roger's words,

> *On this level, there is clarification of who you are, within your own self. In this realm, there is a testing process to see if you are ready to move into the soul realm. If you have been traveling on the etheric realm, you may wake up with the sense, "I've got it! I've really got it!" You won't be able to say what, but you'll know it.*

If language had problems grasping the nature of the etheric, it is even more inadequate to the task of describing the *soul realm*. While not the highest level of the inner realms (i.e., there are levels above the soul level), reaching it is the immediate goal of humankind, in that this is what can break the cycle of reincarnation. All of the levels below the soul are designated as "negative" in comparison with the soul level and higher levels, which are designated as "positive," as in the positive and negative poles of a battery; not as in "good" and "bad." John-Roger says that:

> *The soul realm is your home. If you want to think of it in this way, you are an alien here, in a strange land;*

you may be on the earth, but you are not of the earth. The earth has been designated as the classroom where you learn lessons. When you have finished your lessons, you graduate to other levels of consciousness.

MSIA superimposes a hierarchy of initiations on these levels of being. We live our everyday lives in the physical realm and thus require no formal physical initiation per se; being born is the "initiation" on this level. John-Roger teaches that when one comes in touch with the Mystical Traveler, one experiences an initiation referred to as the astral initiation, which takes place in the dream state.

Most people who become active in MSIA begin their involvement with a series of monthly lessons referred to as Soul Awareness Discourses. Discourses represent more than simply information. MSIA teaches that through studying the monthly lessons, the reader is spiritually linked to the Mystical Traveler Consciousness. The person holding the Traveler Consciousness agrees to assist the reader in clearing karma, which can be released while reading the Discourses. This is a one-to-one agreement made between the Traveler and the Discourse reader. For this reason, MSIA recommends that the Discourses be strictly confidential and not shared with other persons. While this portrayal of what transpires while one is "on Discourses" may strike outsiders as rather odd, it is fully in accord with MSIA's understanding of the relationship between the external (10%) level and the internal (90%) level — externally, all the individual is doing is subscribing to a series of monthly lessons; internally, however, the individual's soul is entering into a spiritual relationship with the Mystical Traveler Consciousness.

After studying the Discourses for two years, one may apply for the first, formal initiation, referred to as the causal initiation.

Thereafter, the aspirant may apply for each of the subsequent initiations — mental, etheric, and soul — contingent upon the individual's maintaining an active involvement in the various levels of lessons available from MSIA headquarters (Soul Awareness Discourses and, when the Discourse series is complete, Soul Awareness Tapes). At the causal initiation, the MSIA student is given a "tone" to utilize in her or his spiritual exercise and receives additional tones with each subsequent initiation. Higher initiations indicate progressively deeper involvement. In another sense, however, all initiates are "soul initiates," although they may not yet be initiated to the soul realm. Ideally, therefore, no student in MSIA should be viewed as being "higher" or "lower" than another.

MSIA's core technique is a kind of meditation involving the mental chanting of one's initiatory tones and attunement to the inner sound, which is the manifestation in consciousness of the Sound Current. John-Roger teaches that this core technique is more active than meditation (in the strict sense). Instead of meditation, MSIA calls its central process spiritual exercise (normally referred to as S.E.s). To cite a relevant passage from J-R's early book, *Inner Worlds of Meditation*:

> *Within MSIA, I teach another dimension to the meditative process, which changes it from a passive technique of "emptying the mind" to an active technique of directing the mind and emotions. I call these active meditations "spiritual exercises," which suggests the activity of exercises combined with the spiritual focus and thrust.*

One of the central goals of MSIA's spiritual practices is to awaken and strengthen the knowledge of each person that their core identity is awareness. In S.E.s, they are able to "witness"

— to calmly observe thoughts, feelings, images, sensations, desires, and modes of identity. For example, an individual who witnesses her body squirming on the seat, feeling anxious, seeing an image of the Eiffel Tower, and thinking thoughts like, I forgot to pay my electric bill; I am really scared Joe doesn't love me anymore; I really have to refocus on chanting and stop spacing out so much; and so forth, learns experientially that the observing consciousness — not the contents of one's mental field — is the essence of one's identity.

MSIA students are encouraged to engage in S.E.s for a period of two hours every day, though many members do so for varying periods, often of lesser duration. More important than the duration of spiritual exercises, however, is the student's presenting himself/herself in devotion to God and making a connection with the Divine — in John-Roger's words, "Even five minutes of devotion to S.E.s can be worth weeks of mechanical repetition." Or as John Morton says in the tape entitled "Blessings, Prayers, and Invocations":

> *Using your devotion to have contact with God, you can move yourself into the knowing that that relationship is sacred, but is also a joyous and magnificent occasion. There is something truly wonderful that goes on when we worship: You are placing yourself before the One that you would most want to be with and see and know and hear and touch . . . to come into that Presence and move beyond the world in consciousness. It doesn't have to be something really specific like what did you see or what were the sounds and colors. It can just be the realization that you are loved, that you are nurtured, that you are taken care of and that you are protected — a chance to re-source and to regenerate.*

Like meditation, spiritual exercises can constitute a challenging discipline that one must work at for a long time before they become comfortable and natural, and there are a number of places in MSIA literature where guidelines and suggestions for the proper practice of S.E.s are given. While some of these guidelines are technical in nature, many are such common sense recommendations as: unplug the phone and put a "do not disturb" sign on the door of your room so that your practice is not interrupted.

During spiritual exercises, initiates mentally chant tones that are keyed to each of the levels. MSIA teaches that when one repeats one's initiatory tones, the Beings who "rule" each world (like the archangels of the Judeo-Christian tradition who represent God in the form of individualized governors or "gods" of each realm) are tuned into and by sympathetic resonance figuratively reach down and pull one up to their level. By traversing the realms while doing S.E.s one is able to build a "bridge" to the higher realms (the golden bridge of consciousness). In John-Roger's words, "Through spiritual exercises, you create a channel, an opening, a tunnel, through which Spirit can convey its wisdom to you."

The practice of spiritual exercises enables students to turn their attention away from the outer realm of the manifested world to the inner realms of the spirit. This redirection of consciousness is the source of MSIA's name, the Movement of Spiritual Inner Awareness. Soul Transcendence — which, according to MSIA literature, is "becoming aware of oneself as a soul and, more than that, as one with God" — is the ultimate goal of MSIA spiritual practices and releases one from the cycle of death and rebirth in which one is trapped, as discussed in a previous chapter.

In terms of the above schema of levels and bodies, the process of reincarnation is one in which the individual loses his/her outermost layer at death, disappears from the physical level, and then reacquires a body at rebirth. We might think of this as being like a sponge diver. Sponge divers put on bulky, spacesuit-like diving suits while collecting sponges. These suits are, in a metaphorical sense, an additional "body." Divers put on this extra body in order to be able to operate at the "liquid" level. After finishing their task in the water and returning to the surface, they divest themselves of their outermost sheath until the next time they need to undertake further work at the "liquid level."

As mentioned earlier, in both Buddhism and Hinduism, life in a corporeal body is viewed negatively as the source of all suffering. Hence the goal is to obtain release from the process of reincarnation. From the perspective of present-day, world-affirming Western society, this vision cannot but appear distinctly unappealing. A modern-day Buddha might respond, however, that our reaction to being confronted with the dark side of life merely shows how insulated we are from the pain and suffering that is so fundamental to human existence. In the contemporary West, for example, we sometimes shut up our elderly and deformed citizens in institutions where we do not have to view them. This stands in marked contrast to the third world, in which it is not uncommon to confront the ravages of disease and mortality on a daily basis. Our situation is, in fact, much like that of the young Gautama (Buddha's given name) in the story of the Four Signs.

According to Buddhist tradition, an astrologer who examined the future Buddha's horoscope immediately after birth asserted that the young prince would eventually become either a world ruler (meaning he would become king of all of India) or a world teacher (in the sense of a religious teacher). The direction — religious or political — the young man would pursue would depend upon whether or not he reflected seriously on the suffering and transitoriness of the human condition. Gautama's father, the king of a small state in what is today southern Nepal, was a worldly man who naturally wanted his son to become a world ruler. As a consequence, he made sure to surround the young man with constant merrymaking and forbade anyone who was elderly or sick to be in the prince's presence.

All went according to plan until about age thirty, when Gautama decided to travel outside of his palace without first informing his parents. On the first day, he happened to see a severely sick person. Upon asking his chariot driver about the man's unusual condition, his servant replied that all people were subject to disease. This troubled the future Buddha. On the second day, he happened to see an exceedingly old man. Upon again inquiring of the chariot driver (who, legend has it, was a demigod in disguise), he discovered that everyone was subject to the aging process. On the third day he saw a corpse, and became really troubled after he was informed that every person eventually met death. Finally, on the fourth day, he saw a sadhu — a holy man who had renounced the world to seek moksha — and resolved that he would also renounce the world and seek liberation. Gautama then left home and years later achieved the goal of release.

But, someone might respond, Why not just try to live life, despite its many flaws, as best one can, avoiding pain and seeking pleasure? Because, Buddha would respond, while we might be able to exercise a certain amount of control over this incarnation, we cannot foresee the circumstances in which our karma would compel us to incarnate in future lives, which might be as a starving child in a war-torn area of the third world. Also, the Buddha would point out, if we closely examine our life, we can see that even the things that seem to bring us our greatest enjoyments also bring us the greatest pain. This aspect of Buddhist thought was embodied in that part of Buddha's system referred to as the Three Marks of Being.

In the first place, Buddha points out, we have to contend with the experiences everyone recognizes as painful — illness, accidents, disappointments, and so forth. Second, the world is in a constant state of change, so even the things we experience as pleasurable do not last and ultimately lead to pain. (Romantic relationships, for example, initially bring us great happiness, but more often than not they end in greater suffering.) And third, because we ourselves are in a constant process of change, we ultimately lose everything we have gained, particularly in the transition we call death.

While MSIA shares Buddhism's basic world view, it focuses less on the negative aspects of life in the physical realm and more on the positive aspects of the individual's release into the soul realm. What comes to mind here is the old saw about there being two basic types of people according to how they regard a partial glass of water: Buddha would say the glass was half-empty; John-Roger would say it was half-full. Congruent with MSIA's more affirmative attitude, human existence in the physical body is not perceived as a purely negative condition. Rather, life in this body is affirmed as an opportunity for soul growth, in the sense that the soul, which is seen as perfect but inexperienced, is here to learn and gain experience. In fact, according to J-R the physical level is the only one from which a soul can spring all the way to the soul realm, so that being here is a great blessing and opportunity. Where early Buddhism's central metaphors suggest the reduction, extraction, dissolution, and eventual elimination of self, MSIA's core images suggest that the spiritual life is a process of exploration, expansion, learning, and healing.

Traditional religions have, further, tended to emphasize the sharp transition from a nonenlightened or nonsaved state to an enlightenment or salvation. In contrast, MSIA and other contemporary schools of metaphysical spirituality emphasize gradual growth, expansion of consciousness, and learning across time, including growth across many different lifetimes. Thus, in contrast with traditional Hinduism and Buddhism — which view reincarnation negatively, as a cycle of suffering out of which one should strive to liberate oneself — in the contemporary metaphysical subculture, reincarnation is viewed positively, as a series of opportunities for expanded spiritual growth. (Though, to be sure, MSIA focuses on ending the cycle of reincarnation.) This gradual spiritual expansion constitutes a kind of evolution of the soul, and the metaphor of spiritual evolution (in the sense of gaining experience) is often expressed in the literature of MSIA and of the New Age subculture more generally.

Rather than an experience of sudden enlightenment, spiritual growth is often likened to healing. Thus, as in many New Age groups, MSIA employs certain techniques of psychoemotional healing as aids to spiritual growth. Some of these are aura balances, innerphasings, and polarity balances — all of which make reference to the human being's nonphysical bodies and/or energies.

The aura is a field of subtle energy that envelops living entities. The basic idea of an envelopment of subtle, vital energy emanating from the body has been widely accepted in many cultures and times. There are records in art and writing of such a belief in ancient India, Egypt, Rome, and Greece. Invisible and undetectable to normal human sight, the aura can be seen by people with the gift of clairvoyance, or "psychic sight." Individuals with such gifts describe the aura as a colorful field that can have rays, streamers, and other distinct phenomena associated with it. The size, brightness, colors, and so forth indicate different things about the individual's emotional and physical state. Clairvoyant healers assert that illness begins as a disturbance in the aura, and that it take months or sometimes even years before a physical illness manifests.

Aura balancing is said to clear the individual's energy field. MSIA offers a series of three aura balances — for the physical aura, the emotional aura, and the mental/spiritual aura. Each balance is said to clear imbalances and strengthen the consciousness so it can better handle everyday stress. Having a balanced aura is also said to contribute to one's creative flow, to assist individuals in having a more accurate perception of themselves and the world, and to help one be more available to the presence of spirit. Many religious traditions, as well as traditional Western occultism, view the aura as emanating from a subtle, nonphysical "body." This subtle body is, as I have already noted, one of several secondary bodies in which the soul is "clothed." Some traditional cultures have gone so far as to map out the anatomy of some of the subtle "energy" body closest to the physical body. The best known of these is Chinese acupuncture. Another tradition with a complex understanding of the subtle body is the Hindu yoga tradition, in which the subtle body is referred to as the *linga sharira.*

Polarity balances are said to balance the energies in the subtle body and to remove blocks so that the flow of energy in the body is enhanced. The effects of releasing these blocks can include more energy, lightness (as though a weight had been lifted), greater attunement to the physical body, and a greater ability to function physically in the world.

Innerphasings are more complex, in that they involve levels of the self beyond the aura and the "energy" body. Innerphasing is said to be able to align the many levels of our consciousness so that we can live in "one accord" with ourselves. In particular, the (mostly unconscious) lower self tends to hang on to habits of behavior and emotion that no longer serve us. Innerphasing creates a "channel of communication" between the conscious self and this lower self (which MSIA calls the "basic self"), so that one can redirect negative or limiting habit-patterns such as compulsive anger, anxiety, overeating, smoking, and so forth into more positive ones, and so that one can establish a closer partnership with the basic self.

Like the New Age in general, and in line with MSIA's growth metaphor, spiritual striving is likened to the process of learning, giving rise to a host of educational images and forms to embody essentially religious meanings. In other words, the dominant "ceremonies" in the metaphysical subculture are workshops, lectures, seminars, and classes rather than worship ceremonies. These educational settings reflect a view of the human condition that sees spiritual development as a gradual learning process, rather than as the kind of abrupt conversion experience that occurs in the midst of traditional Protestant revivals. For this reason, one should be careful to note that MSIA classes, seminars, lectures, and workshops should be regarded as religious activities, structurally comparable to Christian worship services.

In marked contrast to a tradition like Buddhism, MSIA teachings encompass techniques and processes intended as much to improve human life in this world as to promote Soul Transcendence, although Soul Transcendence remains the central and overwhelmingly most important aspect of the Movement. A useful example of this are the so-called PAT Trainings.

In May of 1995, as part of my research on MSIA, I attended an MSIA retreat held in the countryside outside of Woodstock, Illinois. The substance of the retreat was a five-day workshop quaintly referred to as "PAT I" (the first in a series of Peace Awareness Trainings). The gentle, uplifting connotations of "PAT" and "Peace" belie the true nature of this training. If my experience was typical, it should be renamed the "PUNCH," "POKE," or "POUND" training — designations that would alert prospective participants to the fact that "PAT I" was more like a spiritual boot camp than like a bunch of mellow folks hanging out together while sipping cups of herbal tea.

One custom MSIA often integrates into its events is so-called sharings, at which participants stand up and share with the group whatever they wish. After only a few days of PAT, I recall standing up at a sharing and asserting that, "There's a special place in hell for the person who invented this process." Everyone in the room laughed, even the facilitator. I felt as though I was giving voice to the entire group's unspoken feelings. Somewhat later during the same retreat, I stood up and shared that I was comforted by the thought that I would eventually be writing about my experience of this training, and that I would then "get my revenge."

By one of those strange coincidences that make you think there might actually be meaning in the universe after all, Woodstock, Illinois, was where the town-square sequences for the 1994 film *Groundhog Day* were filmed. In *Groundhog Day*, Bill Murray wakes up to find himself caught in a *Star Trek*-like time loop, perpetually reliving the same day over and over again. The core of the movie is constituted by the innumerable strategies Murray's character deploys in his efforts to deal with his entrapment. Over the course of the film, he gradually evolves from a rather nasty prima donna into a nice guy. Finally he is freed from the time loop and, presumably, lives happily ever after.

PAT I is much like *Groundhog Day*. The core technique — which participants promise to discuss only with other PAT veterans (so that future participants won't try to prepare for it, and thus minimize the benefit of the experience) — is redundant in the extreme, forcing one to exhaust all of one's strategies in an effort to derive meaning and insight from an apparently meaningless exercise. For myself (and I can only speak for myself, as different participants have different experiences), the effect was not unlike that of Zen meditation. In Zen

Buddhism, particularly in the Rinzai School of Zen, meditators grapple with a question (a *koan*) that has no logical answer. A well-known example of a koan is the question, "What is the sound of one hand clapping?" Aspirants meditate on the koan, racking their brains for some kind of a solution. Then, in a moment of sudden insight, the answer to the koan flashes across the mind in a kind of mini-enlightenment experience.

My moment of insight occurred late on the third day of the PAT. Not long after my PAT I training, I attempted to describe my experience in a context where my conversation was recorded. That part of the interview reads as follows:

> *I would try different strategies, such as just describing everything I was feeling. And then I would think, Well, I'm not going anywhere with that. So, maybe what I'm supposed to be doing is deep self-analysis. Or maybe I should be entertaining the other person. Or maybe I should . . . What the hell am I supposed to be doing?! My personal experience was like meditating on a Zen koan, and the meditator has to take the koan and meditate on it. And then he comes and says to the Master, "Well, is the answer this? Or this? Or this?" And the Master says, "No!" BAM! [sound of the Master striking the meditator with a stick] "Go do it again!"*
>
> *Eventually, about the third or fourth day, I ran out of strategies. After having exhausted every possible response to the PAT process over the course of the preceding two and a half days — responses ranging from the most profound to the most mundane — I became intensely aware of the mind's omnipresent, reflexive drive to control experience by imposing conceptual order on everything that entered the field of consciousness. It was impossible to have a sponta-*

neous response to the core PAT technique. Even deciding not to respond resulted from a conscious decision. Furthermore, I realized that our experiences are structured by our expectations. This web of expectancy acted like a mental filter, shaping experiences even before entering one's mental field.

What I realized in the end was that everything I was talking about was my trying to anticipate what I was supposed to be doing. It was all mental constructs, and I wasn't able to just *be* there. Even trying simply to describe experiences was just another concept I was operating from. I was following out the program of a certain idea. Basically, there was no way I could ever get away from these programs — these expectancies set up by my ideas and concepts.

As a professional writer and scholar, the conceptual structure between myself and the world that exists beyond ideas and preconceptions was more elaborate than most. Having studied the philosophical traditions of both East and West, I had even read many philosophers — from Nagarjuna to Gadamer — who discussed in exquisite detail how the mind structures and "predigests" experience, always denying us direct experience of the world. I had, however, never really experienced the mind's constant structuring work until the PAT training.

I particularly recall a moment of lucidity while gazing out a window at the leaves and branches of a nearby tree. In the face of the beauty of immediate sensory experience, my various conceptual structures appeared artificial and distant from reality.

There was a moment of enlightenment where I deeply realized that there was an unconceptualized and unconceptualizable reality out there — that all of my concepts are just very artificial — which sort of makes the task of a scholar absurd, ultimately. So I have a keen sense of irony about the kind of task I have set for myself. Here I am writing about MSIA theology, realizing that it is impossible to talk about any of this stuff. But, still, I have to write about something.

I further realized that, if my thoughts were so artificial, then the only thing that held them in place was the force of habit. Why, I asked myself, couldn't things be different? What, ultimately, prevented me from just changing my mind, thinking entirely different thoughts, and having a completely different experience of the world? For a moment, I had an overwhelming experience of human freedom and a sense of infinite possibilities. As J-R says in *The Tao of Spirit:*

> *I'll tell you a secret about this world: it meets you exactly where it finds you and gives you what you present to it.*
>
> *So, if you go out there looking for anger, it will justify your anger.*
> *If you go out there looking for love, it will justify your love.*

For those few moments, I had a deep, experiential realization of the dynamic relationship between human consciousness and the world that made this seemingly simple observation come alive with a depth I had never before experienced.

Later that night while again engaged in the PAT training's central process, my composure broke apart. The essential absurdity of what we were doing overwhelmed me. I started laughing and making silly noises, finally falling off my chair and pounding the floor in an episode of manic laughter. These antics disrupted the session for the other thirty or so people in the room, who quickly joined me in my silliness. Tension from the monotonous technique had been building for days, and everyone welcomed the chance to let down and break free. That night it seemed we had finally scaled the crest of a towering hill, and the balance of the PAT training was a lighter experience for all of us. By the end of the five days, the group had become quite close. We were still, technically, strangers, but we were strangers who now shared a unique experience.

No matter how absurd the PAT training might have showed our everyday lives to be, we all, perhaps paradoxically, came out of the retreat with a renewed vigor for life. For myself, my rather abstract realization about the artificiality of our conceptual schemes made me aware of how I was expending my entire life working with ideas, and how, as a consequence, I was distant from living. I left Woodstock determined to spend more time enjoying my life and, more particularly, enjoying time with my wife and daughter.

The PAT training is but one of the many workshops, seminars, classes, and trainings available through MSIA. The MSIA parallel to a Christian service, in the sense of the basic meeting one attends as an active Church member, is the home gathering. Home gatherings take the form of a taped seminar — a meeting built around a tape of J-R to which the group listens. Live seminars are normally public talks by John Morton or J-R, though other members have been given the authorization to hold such seminars. Members need not, of course, attend any such function. Like Christians who never attend church but who pray and study scripture in private, MSIA folks need only do their spiritual exercises and study Discourses to be regarded as active students.

Almost all events that do not take the form of home gatherings or live seminars are regarded as falling under the auspices of Peace Theological Seminary and College of Philosophy (often abbreviated PTS), MSIA's educational wing. In recent years, PTS has begun to offer a full curriculum of courses — courses that can, if one has the proper prerequisites, lead to a

Master of Theology degree. One should be careful to note, however, that, unlike traditional Christian denominations, graduation from MSIA's seminary is NOT a prerequisite for ordination as an MSIA minister. Furthermore, MSIA ministers, unlike their Christian counterparts, are not primarily church leaders. Rather, each minister develops his or her own ministry of service. Anyone who has been a member in good standing for two years can apply to become a minister, and over half of all active participants have been ordained.

In regard to its educational outreach, certain aspects of MSIA have changed significantly over the years. Thus, for example, the first educational institution to emerge out of the group — an institution now called the University of Santa Monica (USM) — has since separated itself as a distinct school catering primarily to non-MSIA members. Similarly, in the 1970s, certain MSIA participants developed educational seminars — Insight Training Seminars (later Insight Transformational Seminars) — in order to provide an intense transformational experience. These seminars can be compared to est (Erhard Seminar Trainings) and Lifespring, although Insight's emphasis was always on the ability to move beyond self-imposed limitations rather than on the intense confrontations that characterized est. Insight Seminars, like USM, has since become completely distinct from MSIA.

The core of MSIA's teaching is embodied in the Soul Awareness Discourses. The Discourses are a series of monthly lessons — lessons which are to be read, digested, and reflected upon across the course of a month's time. At present, 5000+ people study with the Church of the Movement of Spiritual Inner Awareness, which means, minimally, that they subscribe to the Soul Awareness Discourses. Somewhat more than half of these are in the United States, and the rest are in other countries, principally Mexico and Latin America; England, France, and Spain; Australia; Canada; and Nigeria.

The first year of Discourses is said to contain all of the basic information. J-R has stated, perhaps rhetorically, that if a person really "got" the first Discourse, that would be enough (there are a total of 144 Discourses). The Discourses, however, represent more than simply information. As mentioned earlier in this chapter, MSIA teaches that through reading the monthly lessons, the reader, especially if he or she is studying toward initiation, is connected in a deeper way to the Mystical Traveler Consciousness.

As evidence for the "mystical" efficacy of the Discourses, I have heard innumerable stories about how people read something in their Discourses that seemed to speak directly to their situation and that affected the course of their lives. Later, however, when they went back to try to find the particular passage that had had such an impact on them, they were unable to find it again — implying that the passage in question had appeared in their consciousness at the time, and that it was not actually a permanent part of the Discourse booklet. John-Roger has described this phenomenon in the following words:

> *Discourses become the point of contact for the Spirit inside of you and a point of attunement with the Mystical Traveler Consciousness. As people read them, they say, "I hear your voice reading inside of me, and I'll hear you tell me other things." Then they'll tell somebody, "Well, in Discourse 22, J-R said so-and-so." "But that's not in Discourse 22." They [say], "Yeah, it is." They go back and read it, and it's not. Later I get a letter from them in which they say, "Why did you change the material in that Discourse? I read it; it was there and then you removed it!" It's like, I haven't been to your house. I didn't remove it. How do you explain it?*

The Discourses provide the reader with introductory meta-physical information about such things as the Traveler and the Light, but in line with MSIA's more affirmative attitude toward life — they also provide basic guidelines on how to walk the spiritual path in the midst of everyday life. This is reflected in the titles of the basic Soul Awareness Discourses, which range from Discourses on the nature of the Mystical Traveler Consciousness to essays on acceptance and responsibility.

If I had to summarize the central thrust of these teachings about life in the world, I would say that MSIA holds out to its students the paradoxical ideal of detached engagement:

> *The message of MSIA is that God is in Heaven, that there are greater realms, that you don't have to die to experience them, and that you can know the divine reality while you live on this earth.*

John-Roger has, further, described the ideal of detached engagement as "living in a portable paradise":

> *Guidelines have been presented by the Masters of all the ages, guidelines for living your life in the Light of the Christ, in the Light of your own consciousness, free of suffering. These guidelines help you handle yourself in this world. Not handling this world too well does not stop your spiritual growth, but you'll be happier if you are handling it rather well. So if you want to be happier, it is your responsibility to learn those things that make it easier to live a successful, uplifting life here.*

As long as we hold on to our attachments and continue to nurse our pains, we will never really be able to gain release from this world and maintain our consciousness in the Soul realms. However, once proper detachment is gained, we are also free to enjoy ourselves in this world, the world of our everyday experience. In J-R's words from *The Tao of Spirit*:

Do you accomplish a lot here?
Probably not.
Then what's the value here?
The value here is not to accomplish a lot,
because it's all been accomplished.

Your job is to become aware of the divine presence
within you,
which you are,
and to use this level to spring into higher
consciousness.

That's what this level is about.
It's the springboard,
not the place you stay in.

Your job is easy.
You can extract yourself from any situation that you
want to,
if you're willing to pay the sacrifice
of giving up your greeds
and your pride,
and your lusts,
and your envy,
and your ego,
and just live purely in the moment.

5

STEPPING ONTO THE PATH:
WHY PEOPLE JOIN

Like so many other people in the sixties, I was searching. I found my vocation as an actress when I was quite young. I combined this career with my involvement in the counterculture. I appeared in Andy Warhol movies and was touted as the world's "First Nude Actress." Suddenly I was the most "in" thing happening. They had me in Vogue Magazine *and* Harper's Bazaar. *I was on the "Merv Griffin Show" and the "Dick Cavett Show." Being the first nude actress in the country, much less the world, was really quite a happening.*

It was sometime in the winter of 1994–95, and I was attending an introductory MSIA seminar, listening to actress Susan Kelly (not her real name). Kelly is a humorous, entertaining speaker, who is especially engaging when talking out of personal experience. That particular evening, she talked about the experiences that had brought her to John-Roger's spiritual movement.

The daughter of American aristocrats, her mother was the fashion editor of *Life Magazine*. Like many other young people coming of age in the 1960s, Kelly rebelled against her upper-class background to join the emerging counterculture. Kelly attributed the "craziness" of the acting profession with prompting her to seek God. Initially, she became involved with Swami Satchitananda, even joining his staff and teaching yoga classes for his organization.

Kelly's first encounter with John-Roger occurred in 1972, when she was living in southern California. On the fortieth day of a carrot juice fast, she was hospitalized for an inability to void urine. Unable to determine the cause of the problem, her doctors planned a dangerous operation on her spine. Kelly, however, had other ideas. After convincing them to give her an outpass, she walked out of the hospital:

> *Finally, when I'm far enough away from Century Hospital, I see this newspaper stand. One of the papers catches my eye because it doesn't look like a normal newspaper. So I look and, by God, there's Satya Sai Baba on the cover, and he's got his arm around this guy. And the guy's name is John-Roger.*
>
> *So suddenly I'm jealous of this guy because he knows Sai Baba — this high, holy person I've been trying to get to come to this country. So the next thing I know, I take a copy of this newspaper — I think it was called* The Movement *— and suddenly I experience this wave of energy. I just got all blissed out of my little head, and I came back to the hospital and I was fine. So that was my introduction to John-Roger.*

While the particulars of Kelly's story are unique, the more general scenario — joining a religious group in the wake of a spiritual experience — is a typical, though certainly not a universal, pattern.

As part of my research, I collected demographic data via a short questionnaire (described in more detail in a subsequent chapter). One of the statistics this survey collected was data on how people become involved in MSIA. Most people become involved with a religious group — whether traditional or non-traditional — through family and friendship networks. Thus, I was not surprised to find the same pattern among MSIA participants (current and past), over half of whom were introduced to the Movement by family or friends.

This statistic, however, tells us only how members were brought into contact with MSIA, and not specifically what attracted them to hang around after the initial contact. In Kelly's case, for example, her initial contact was via an initially impersonal encounter with *The Movement* newspaper. It was, however, the spiritual experience (described as a "wave of energy" in the above passage) accompanying her examination of the paper that prompted her to regard John-Roger as more than just another spiritual teacher.

One of the few open-ended items on the survey form asked respondents to discuss briefly how they had become involved in MSIA. Some members provided more detail than others. In one particularly rich account, the respondent met John-Roger during a trip in Egypt and subsequently, while taking a bath, had a remarkable spiritual experience related to J-R:

> *A ball of light formed over my head. Then the ball exploded and I knew everything and saw all my lifetimes with this man (Roger Hinkins). . . . When I stepped out of the bath, the words in my mind were, "THE SAME" — "HE IS THE SAME." I went to*

> *dinner and a clairvoyant friend said to me, ". . . our Spiritual Master is on this trip! I know because I recognize him as the same as the one in my heart." I knew who he meant because of what I had just experienced. I've been active in MSIA ever since.*

More than a few other respondents reported spiritual experiences in the initial stages of their affiliation with MSIA, though in most cases these were less dramatic. By reflecting on such experiences we can understand one reason why people join non-mainstream religions, which is that many alternative religions hold out the possibility of life-transforming experiences — experiences that, to a greater or lesser extent, help one to drop the burden of the past and be reborn into a new and more complete life.

The mainstream Protestant denominations — Methodists, Baptists, and Presbyterians — once offered the seeker life-transforming experiences in the context of revivals and camp meetings. But as these religious bodies settled down into comfortable accommodation with the surrounding (largely secular) society, they lost their intensity. One result of this accommodation was that revivals and camp meetings — and the accompanying intense religious experiences — were relegated to a quaint and mildly embarrassing chapter in denominational histories.

Those of us who are happily adjusted to the social-cultural mainstream often have a difficult time understanding intense religiosity. Academics have not been exempt from this tendency. An earlier generation of sociologists of religion, seemingly obsessed with the issue of conversion to non-mainstream "sect" groups, gave excessive attention to explaining why individuals become involved in such churches.

If, however, rather than dwelling on strange externals, we change our point of focus and attempt to really look at what might attract someone to an alternative religion, such involvement is not really difficult to understand. Is the attraction of transformational experiences, for example, really so hard to comprehend? What if we actually could let go of the burden of our past and be reborn as new people? Such transformation may or may not be attainable, but the attractiveness of the possibility is certainly understandable. Many non-mainstream religions — conservative Christian sects included — hold out the promise of such life-changing experiences. Religious experience is, however, only one aspect of the spiritual life, and only one of the factors that attract individuals to deeper religious involvement.

Among the many approaches to religious studies, one of the older, yet still useful, scholarly analyses was articulated by the influential historian of religion, Joachim Wach. The primary core of religion, according to Wach, is religious experience. Religious experience, in turn, is expressed in at least three ways:

> In a community (church, ashram, etc.)
> In a doctrine (theology, world view, etc.)
> In a "cultus" (ritual, gathering, etc.)

To understand Wach's analysis with a simple example, let us imagine how my experience at the Spring Renewal described in Chapter Three might become the basis for a new religious group.

In the first place, it is easy to conceive of how a community might emerge out of the shared experience of the forgiveness exercise. I spent a week at the Spring Renewal. The exercise took place on the morning of the third day, if I remember correctly. Up until that point, I did not feel like I was really a part of the group: I was from the mainland (most of the participants were island residents). I also tended to keep a reserved distance as part of my academic persona. After the exercise, this changed dramatically. I became quite close to a number of the participants and clearly recall wishing we could just continue to live together in the YMCA camp at which the gathering was held. This feeling of community is a natural result of shared experiences, and it is relatively easy to see how these feelings might form the basis of a spiritual fellowship.

The forgiveness exercise was also such a cleansing, uplifting experience that it is not difficult to see how it might form the basis for a regular gathering — for a "ritual," in the broadest sense of the word. In other words, we can well imagine how the people who had shared the experience might agree to meet on a regular basis and reenact the exercise in order to recapture the original experience. This would become our rough equivalent of a "church service."

Finally, it is also possible to see how the experience might constitute the basis for a new theology: The Sufi teacher who led the group initially provided us with a few quasi-theological notions, such as the "fall-from-Eden" story of the eclipse of matriarchy by "evil" patriarchs. If we extend this quasi-theology to the exercise, perhaps the group experience of forgiveness might become our new religion's equivalent of a salvation experience that restored our souls to prepatriarchal paradise. This application of Wach's analysis, while greatly oversimplified, should give us a basic feel for the fundamental constituents of religion. In outline form, these constituents are:

> Spiritual experience
> Community
> Doctrine/idea system
> Gatherings/rituals

Each of these four components sheds light on how individuals become involved in nontraditional religions.

As I have already indicated, many MSIA participants become involved in the group in the wake of a spiritual experience. This factor is particularly emphasized in older academic literature about religious conversion. In this body of literature, the suddenness of the experience is stressed. The implicit or explicit paradigm is the Damascus Road experience, in which the apostle Paul was knocked off his horse by a bolt out of the blue, confronted by Jesus, and converted on the spot. Contemporary studies have found, however, that it rarely works that way. Rather, in most cases, individuals just gradually "drift" into a religious group until they cross a barely perceptible line between outsider and insider, undergoing a series of "mini-conversions" en route.

The stepwise progression involved in such conversions was reflected in a number of the responses to the MSIA survey. To cite one in which the respondent had a number of spiritual experiences before joining:

> *I had an inner experience of the Traveler's voice. I knew the voice to be that of John-Roger as I'd heard it once at a taped seminar in 1974. I'd gone to [the seminar] because I'd had a mystical experience, believe it or not, when I saw a poster about MSIA. I was very surprised by the experience and very reluctant to get involved. I had a powerful inner experience at the first taped seminar I attended and felt scared. I stayed away for about five years until the next inner experience.*

Other participants come to a seminar, have no remarkable experiences, but keep coming back because they like the people or the teachings. They may even begin subscribing to Discourses with no particular intention of making MSIA their spiritual home. However, if they continue returning, they eventually step across a threshold between "them" and "us," and, before they know it, begin identifying themselves as participants in the Movement. The majority of respondents did not report spiritual experiences as playing a role in their "conversion" to MSIA; for example:

> *A friend of mine in Santa Barbara and I were searching for a Master in the physical body. She attended an MSIA seminar, then called and told me I might want to check it out. I went to Conference #3 in 1971. After John-Roger's summer traveling, I started going to seminars in El Monte, then moved back to Santa Barbara in November. I heard about Discourses, and started them in December 1971. There were no great fireworks or revelations, just this quiet inner peace that let me know I was on the right path.*

There were also a number of people who experienced what might be labeled "minor" spiritual experiences. Thus one respondent visited an acquaintance who "said J-R's name and showed me his photo." This respondent then felt his "heart expand." As a result of this experience, he began regularly attending MSIA seminars. Another respondent was meditating and "saw J-R inside; then I knew MSIA was my path."

Yet other respondents reported having dreams that played a role in their becoming involved in MSIA. Several respondents, for example, dreamed about J-R before meeting him. I was personally interested in these accounts because, as I related in the introduction, a dream experience had provided me with a key for understanding the Movement in the initial stages of my research:

> *I met some ministers from Australia who gave me a* Wealth 101 *tape. J-R and John Morton showed up in a dream that evening (I did not know either of them*

personally). I recognized J-R, but did not recognize John Morton. Later I saw a photo and realized it was the same person. This intrigued me.

Other respondents described roughly similar experiences; for example:

I met some people who worked with John-Roger. I had a dream in which John-Roger appeared (before I knew what he looked like or what he did). I then met J-R in person and the part of me seeking someone with greater awareness recognized a greater aware-ness in him. I chose to listen to him and check out his teachings.

Moving even further away from the realm of unusual spir-itual phenomena, but still within the arena of direct experi-ence, some respondents reported that they initially became interested in MSIA as a result of meeting members who impressed them in some way; for example:

I began massage therapy with a woman in 1977, who was, and still is, a minister in the Movement (MSIA). Her gifts continually opened my eyes and my heart, although she never proselytized, and only spoke of her faith in response to my questions.

Other respondents described parallel experiences with MSIA participants; for example:

While living in New York I met a person who seemed "at peace." This is quite an accomplishment for liv-ing in that city. His friends (who I later found were in MSIA as well) also had this peace. I became interested.

Closely related to the phenomenon of becoming involved in MSIA via an exceptionally "together" individual is the pattern of being attracted to the group as a consequence of the strong fellowship among MSIA participants.

More generally, the community dimension of any religious group is the key element in initially attracting new members. We live in a society that would have been an alien world to our ancestors. Surrounded by masses of people, we rarely know the names of our closest neighbors. In traditional societies, by way of contrast, everyone in a particular village knew everyone else and took care of everyone else: If, for instance, you saw someone have an accident, you didn't call 911; instead you ran over and helped out as best you could. Some churches and most alternative religions recreate this kind of community among their members.

The fellowships that come into being around churches are, in a certain sense, second families. In modern society, our families are not the close emotional units they were in traditional societies. A small religious group many times recreates the sense of belonging to a family. If one has never experienced the closeness of a traditional family, it is easy to understand how the sense of belonging to a family unit would be attractive and even healing.

The sense of having found a very attractive community of people came through in a number of different ways in the MSIA survey. One respondent reported that when he came through the door of MSIA headquarters he "was instantly struck by the loving energy — even before meeting one person." Another person reported being "really impressed by the goodness of these people. There was a certain energy about them that I found to be very loving and kind — they also laughed a lot."

A metaphor that was frequently employed when respondents explained why they joined was that they felt "at home" with the Movement almost immediately after encountering MSIA; for example: "When I discovered MSIA, I felt like I was 'home.'" The feeling of at-home-ness can, of course, have different shades of meaning, not all of which connote feeling part of a community of people. In other words, one may have a feeling of at-home-ness with the teachings and practices rather than with the community. There were, however, a significant number of respondents whose expression of at-home-ness clearly carried the sense of having found a community of spiritual brothers and sisters. This set of respondents emphasized the experience of feeling accepted and unconditionally loved by MSIA members; for example:

> *He [an MSIA minister] shared such a spirit of loving and unconditional giving with me, my socks were blown off. That [experience] began my journey on this path, which has brought me a profound sense of relief, as I know I had been looking for something for many years. Coming into MSIA was truly like coming home.*

However, as important as the fellowship dimension is for understanding the attractiveness of MSIA, it should be pointed out that some individuals are acutely aware that many participants are with the organization for primarily social purposes. In a few cases, survey respondents explicitly noted that their involvement was based on other factors; for example:

> *I am "in the Movement" because of the inner experiences I have had. I do not utilize any of the classes for social purposes.*

Another respondent, whom I cited in the introduction, stated that:

*I chose MSIA . . . because of my own inner experi-
ence, not necessarily the John-Roger seminars or
Discourses or the group connection, but because of
what I experienced as an individual consciousness.*

While most Discourse subscribers participate in MSIA
events, one can be a member in good standing entirely through
the mail without ever seeing another MSIA person, except during initiations. Thus, as powerful of a factor as fellowship is in
understanding the involvement of many participants, it can be
overstressed.

Two other important factors are MSIA's teachings and the
general world view of MSIA. In a traditional society, beliefs
about the ultimate nature of the universe are largely taken for
granted. In contemporary society, by way of contrast, nothing
can be taken for granted except death and taxes. We are taught
to be "nice" by our school system, but this moral teaching is
not grounded in an ultimate source of value. We are also
instructed in the basic skills necessary to operate in society, but
public school teachers are quiet about the greater questions of
death, purpose, and the meaning of life.

We may place a positive or a negative evaluation on this
relativistic education, but in any case we have to acknowledge
that our culture's ambiguous approach to socialization departs
radically from the socialization strategies of earlier societies.
The results of this ambiguity may be liberating to some people,
but to others it is confusing. Without some kind of ultimate
grounding, this is necessarily the case. While ethical teachings
within different spiritual movements vary widely, they generally share the trait of grounding morality in the Divinity.

Once one has stable criteria for what is good and true, this
clarity and stability can then free one to go about the business
of working, loving, and living life without debilitating anxieties about transcendent meaning and value. There is a song

that Way International (a nontraditional Christian group) members sing called "Standing on Solid Ground," and I think this title captures the flavor of what I am trying to call attention to. Or, as one respondent to the MSIA survey wrote, "I have a solid foundation inside to draw on."

Only a relative handful of survey respondents emphasized what we might call the "intellectual" dimension of MSIA teachings as the primary factor in their initial attraction to the Movement. One respondent in this category wrote that:

> *I was very impressed with MSIA's philosophy. It was the most advanced, profound religion I had ever been exposed to.*

Another respondent praised the teachings as the "highest" on the planet, though in the same breath was careful not to depreciate other teachings:

> *The Mystical Traveler's teaching is, in my opinion, the highest teaching available on the planet today. This is not meant to imply that all the other teachings it has been my privilege to encounter are not also great teachings, or that the mystery teachings of the past in India and Egypt were not of the highest, but only to state that at the present time, this is it!*

More often than not, when respondents mentioned MSIA's teachings it was in terms of the resonance between themselves and the teachings, rather than to remark on their philosophical profundity; for example:

> *I found in MSIA teachings [what] I already believed in yet could find no one else that put it in words and print—I found my truth.*

The impression that, for most participants, the attraction to MSIA is predominately nondiscursive is reinforced by the fact that very few people became involved in the Movement as a direct result of reading John-Roger's books (a finding that surprised me, considering that J-R is a *N.Y. Times* bestselling author, with over a million copies of his books sold). In my survey of 500 current and former members, only two mentioned such books as being primary factors in prompting their participation in the Movement.

Part of the issue here is that a significant percentage of MSIA's basic teachings are not unique to John-Roger, so that no great leap is required to make the transition from some other group in the New Age/metaphysical spectrum to MSIA. Many people, for example, came to MSIA already convinced of the truth of the notions of reincarnation, karma, and the idea that the ultimate goal of life is to escape the cycle of death and rebirth. The more specific issue around which "conversion" occurs is an individual's accepting the notion that MSIA is the best path to enlightenment for himself/herself.

This pattern is not unusual. It is infrequently the case that people without a prior disposition become deeply involved in an intensive religious group. If they do, they rarely remain for any length of time. In *The Making of a Moonie*, a benchmark study by the eminent British sociologist Eileen Barker, evidence was presented which supported the assertion that people who remain affiliated with the Unification Church for more than a few years were already grappling with some of the issues addressed by Unification theology long before they encountered that movement. This finding can be extrapolated to other religious groups.

People join alternate religions for the same sorts of reasons one would join any other religion, namely fellowship, a satisfying belief system, and so forth. When these needs are no longer being fulfilled in an acceptable manner, people leave, much as one would leave an unsatisfying marriage. The majority of people who responded to the questionnaire had been seeking an appropriate spiritual path for many years before encountering MSIA. The following excerpt from one of the surveys is not atypical:

> *Before MSIA, I was interested in meditation and yoga at a Kundalini Ashram. I lived there for approximately six months, and then spent a short time with Stephen Gaskin's "The Farm" group. I also studied with Guru Maharaji and went to India. I spent a month there. I also directed a choir with a metaphysical group originating in France.*

Within the metaphysical/New Age subculture, this kind of sequential experimentation with one religious group after another is not unusual. Sociologists of religion have even coined a phrase for this pattern — the "conversion career" — meaning that the overall pattern of such individuals' spiritual lives is switching from one group to another.

However, the problem with this phrase as well as with the whole project of examining spiritual experimentation in the New Age subculture through the perspective of prior research on conversion in traditional religions is that "conversion" implies a rejection of one's earlier religious group as false while simultaneously embracing one's new faith as true. This is based on a tendency within traditional religions to emphasize the sharp transition from a nonenlightened or nonsaved state to enlightenment or salvation. In contrast, contemporary occult/metaphysical spirituality emphasizes gradual growth, expansion of consciousness, and learning across time, including growth across different lifetimes.

This gradual spiritual expansion constitutes a kind of evolution of the soul, and the metaphor of spiritual evolution is often expressed in the literature of this subculture. As a result, one's earlier involvements are not viewed as dead ends on the path to enlightenment, but, rather, as stepping stones, appropriate for the stage one was in at the time. Thus another MSIA seeker, in her contribution to an early (1974) compilation entitled *Across the Golden Bridge*, described her pre-MSIA journey in the following words:

> *I studied Unity, Physiciana, Seekers of Truth, and became a 4th degree initiate, and then studied Divine Truth and Divine Science for three or four years. I was a doctor and licensed in the New Thought Movement, and a licensed minister in the Spiritualist Church, and also in Practical Christianity. From each of these groups I gained a deeper understanding, but something was missing.*

As reflected in the above passage, this person's experiences of other groups are viewed as incomplete rather than as false — as partial truths that led up to, and prepared the way for, her "conversion" to MSIA. This passage also reflects the dominant metaphor used to describe the process of spiritual evolution: learning.

The tendency to utilize educational discourse and learning metaphors to embody essentially religious meanings is pervasive within the New Age/metaphysical subculture. For example, in the introduction to John-Roger's *The Way Out Book*, J-R talks about life experience being the "teacher" that prepares us to "graduate" from the cycle of death and rebirth. In addition, as I have stated in Chapter Four, the dominant "ceremonies" in this subculture are workshops, lectures, seminars, and classes rather than worship ceremonies per se.

For some participants, the pattern of sampling one teaching after another does not stop after they join MSIA. John-Roger's teachings are tolerant and open-ended — an openness

one member described as a lack of "religious walls."
Furthermore, J-R is careful not to denounce other religious
groups as false (although he does suggest that a serious student
study with only one spiritual teacher in order not to split
his/her energy and in order to give the teacher a fair chance of
working with the student). As a consequence, members feel
free to experiment with non-MSIA spiritual techniques and
paths. In the words of one respondent:

> *MSIA is the only set of teachings I have found to sat-*
> *isfactorily answer all life questions, and also feels*
> *right to participate. I have continued to sample other*
> *spiritual paths as a check that I'm still on the right*
> *path for me. I use a scientific approach to verify the*
> *correctness of my choice of spiritual association.*

In a couple of cases, respondents expressed dissatisfaction
with the Movement, indicating that they were ready to drop
their MSIA affiliation as soon as something else more attractive came along. Unsurprisingly, even people who had left
MSIA tended to view their membership period positively, as a
learning experience. In addition to current participants, questionnaires were also sent to people who had formerly been
active in the group. Out of the 53 ex-members who responded, most felt they benefited in one way or another from their
participation in the Movement. This feeling of having benefited from involvement was explicitly measured by an item on
the questionnaire that asked respondents if their MSIA
involvement had helped or hurt them:

> *How has your involvement in MSIA influenced your*
> *life, for better or for worse?*

Responses to this questionnaire item are tabulated in Table 5.1 below.

Table 5.1 — Better/Worse for the Experience

	Count	Percent
Better	38	71.1
Worse	4	7.8
Mixed	3	5.7
Neither	6	11.3
N/R	2	3.8

With almost three-fourths of the sample willing to assert unambiguously that they feel they are better off for having been participants in MSIA, it is easy to see how so few ex-members felt a need to castigate the Movement, the teachings, or the founder. This situation is perfectly understandable if we realize that most of the people who have left MSIA still consider themselves "on the path," in the larger sense, and continue to participate in some form of metaphysical/New Age spirituality. Such people thus regard their membership period as part of their larger quest, and, as a consequence, positively value the time and energy they invested in MSIA.

The pattern of responses to another questionnaire item that assessed the value of the membership period reinforces this interpretation. This item asked ex-member respondents to imaginatively place themselves back in time at the point where they initially became involved in MSIA:

If you could be transported back to the time you began your involvement with MSIA, you would probably:

1. Do it all over again with few or no changes
2. Do it all over again with many changes
3. Not get so deeply involved
4. Not get involved at all

Responses to this questionnaire item are tabulated in Table 5.2 below.

Table 5.2 — Would You Do It All Over Again?

	Count	Percent
1	32	60.4
2	5	9.4
3	5	9.4
4	7	13.2
N/R	4	7.5

Here once again we have an exaggerated pattern of response. In this particular case, the great majority of the sample (more than three-fifths) assert that, if they had their membership period to do over again, they would "do it all over again with few or no changes."

The ex-member survey form also contained an open-ended item that asked respondents how their involvement in MSIA had influenced their lives, for better or for worse. Parallel to responses from current members indicating that their earlier affiliations had prepared them for MSIA, ex-members tended to view MSIA as a prior stage in their development; for example, to cite from one questionnaire: "I view MSIA as a preparatory phase for what I am doing now." Also, as we might have anticipated, some former participants couched their responses in terms of what they had learned; for example:

> *One of the most useful things I learned was about karma — that our soul is here to learn and experience things that we incarnate onto this planet to do. It has helped me not to be judgmental of other people and myself.*

Another way in which the term "conversion" carries connotations inappropriate for interpreting organizations like MSIA is that such movements are not conversionist in the traditional sense. A general belief in the New Age/metaphysical subculture is that, in J-R's words, "not one soul will be lost." In other words, in sharp contrast to Christianity and certain other traditional faiths, no one is going to be damned to hell for eternity. If not a single soul will be lost, there is, as a consequence, no burning need to "bring everyone into the fold," at least not immediately.

If anything, MSIA's spiritual atmosphere seems to be permeated by an anticonversionist ethic. I received the impression that if anyone were to attempt to collar strangers and bring them to MSIA events, he or she would be censured by other members, or, at the very least, perceived as not embodying the spirit of the Movement. The anticonversionist ethic was reflected in the MSIA questionnaire in a number of ways. For instance, at least a dozen survey respondents reported that, far from experiencing proselytization, they had to twist their contact person's arm before he/she revealed his/her religious affiliation.

Furthermore, MSIA's anticonversionist ethic was often cited as a significant (though never the primary) factor in attracting people to the Movement. This "conversion aversion" was described by several survey respondents as "noninflictive"; for example:

I have appreciated the community of MSIA and feel comfortable around the people and the noninflictive approach.

MSIA's noninflictive approach flows out of its perceived acceptance of human diversity. In the words of one respondent:

One of the key concepts which touched me deeply was hearing J-R say one evening that, "There are as many roads (paths) to God as there are beings on this planet."

With the notion of human diversity at the core of the Movement's teachings, it follows that MSIA can be the appropriate path for only a certain number of people. In line with this idea, John-Roger has said that those who will meet up with the Traveler in this lifetime "have it marked on them."

Thus, as I have heard many participants articulate in a variety of ways, the individuals whom the Movement is meant to attract will find their way to the teachings. When these people stumble across MSIA, they will recognize that they have found their spiritual "home" and will eventually join the Movement.

At the same time, people for whom there is no preexisting resonance with MSIA should not be persuaded to participate, no matter how universal and wholesome one might feel the Movement to be. In most cases, such people will affiliate only briefly and then leave.

This aspect of the teachings leads to an ambivalence about the Movement's growth. Participants are generally happy and want to share their happiness, but at the same time do not want to "inflict" their beliefs on others. This has led to, among other things, a Movement-wide ambivalence about growth. In the 1970s, MSIA expanded rapidly until it had grown to about five thousand members. At that point, growth in total numbers stopped. Over the years people have come and gone, while the overall membership figure has remained about the same.

In terms of this nonexpansion, MSIA presents a profile of being like a traditional lineage in the Hindu tradition centered around a guru and his intimate disciples. Normally, this kind of movement does not attempt to grow beyond a close community of teacher and students. Using this model as a lens through which to view MSIA, it is not surprising that the group has essentially the same number of members as it did twenty years ago. This pattern sharply contrasts with the media portrayal of MSIA as an aggressively expansionist organization out to convert as many members as possible.

The general sense of open-endedness within MSIA allows participants to drop in and out of active membership in the organization, resulting in a kind of "revolving door" phenomenon that one rarely encounters in other small religious groups. As John-Roger once informed me, "People come in and out of the Movement as circular doors. Some are there for a week, some a month. They leave for five to ten years and return as though they never left." J-R has also pointed out that more than a few people who would be regarded as "ex-members" from an organizational perspective continue to actively maintain the spiritual practices they learned while participants in MSIA: "Many of the people who have 'left' are still doing the meditations and establishing their Light and Sound connections, and the only one knowing all of that is the Mystical Traveler."

As I bring this chapter to a close, I should note a number of other factors influencing certain respondents' initial affiliation with MSIA. One of these was that at least three survey respondents were adult children of MSIA members. Given the freedom to become involved or to stay away from the organization by their parents, these individuals chose to join the "fold"; for example:

> *My parents became involved when I was two. They have always encouraged me to explore other religions, however, which I have done. It wasn't until recently that I decided MSIA was for me.*

I could not determine if this pattern was typical or atypical of individuals raised in the Movement, since this was not something that the survey specifically addressed.

Another factor for some members was that John-Roger had been their high school teacher; for example:

> *I have known about MSIA since high school, when John-Roger (then Mr. Roger Hinkins) was my English teacher. About two years ago I was reminded of MSIA by a series of what I call significant events, so I decided to check it out.*

Only a relative handful of currently active participants had J-R as a high school teacher.

Finally, more than a few respondents indicated that one of the factors that attracted them to MSIA was the organization's emphasis on the Christ. This initially surprised me, as the Movement departs markedly from traditional Christianity. Theologically, MSIA's Christology is comparable to the Christology found in many metaphysical religions. (From MSIA's perspective, Jesus was a Mystical Traveler.)

While Christology (the theological interpretation of the person and work of Christ) is not at the core of MSIA's teaching, members nevertheless generally regard themselves as "followers of the Christ Consciousness," as I stated in a previous chapter. And while John-Roger feels free to draw upon all traditions, he most often draws upon the teaching and example of Jesus. A number of survey respondents found this tendency comforting; for example:

> *What I was taught as a child, within a traditional Protestant setup, has "come alive." Jesus, the Christ, and his teachings mean so much to me, and MSIA has helped me in the journey.*

For at least a dozen respondents, a factor attracting them to MSIA was its "Christian" aspect. One should also note, however, that several other respondents reported being "turned off" by this emphasis, or, at least, by John-Roger's Christian languaging of certain concepts. One respondent, for example, reported having difficulty stomaching "words like Christ and Holy Spirit," though she became involved in spite of MSIA's Christian dimension.

6

BACK TO SCHOOL:
LIVING IN THE LIGHT

The earth has been designated as the classroom where you learn lessons. [Y]ou're . . . in a continual learning process, which will bring forth that which is for your highest good. When you have finished your lessons, you graduate to other levels of consciousness.
—John-Roger

I had taken off for a stroll in the late afternoon. The dense forest spread out across the rolling hills like a frozen green ocean. Lost in thought within the stillness of the woods, a distant rumble of thunder roused me from my reverie. Glancing upward through the canopy of leaves, I was startled by the sight of dark, thick, rapidly-approaching rain clouds. While the path I was traveling was unfamiliar, I intuitively knew it would lead to shelter. I quickly picked up my pace from a leisurely stroll to a brisk walk.

The thunderclaps soon became louder and more insistent. The treetops began to sway in response to the approaching storm. Within a matter of minutes, what had begun as a light breeze grew to become a gale-force storm. By now I was running through the woods. Black clouds blocked out the light of the sun, and I could almost taste the moisture in the cold gusts of wind. As I broke out of the woods into a clearing, the first raindrops began falling around me. The rain fell in heavy beads of water that made hard plopping sounds as they hit.

I found myself running as fast as my legs could carry me toward what appeared to be the ruins of an ancient temple on the other side of the clearing. However, the wall of water sweeping across the forest reached me before I was able to reach the shelter of the ruins. Without slowing my pace, I peered through the gray veil of the heavy thundershower, seeking some outcropping or other surviving part of the structure that might shelter me from the onslaught of rain. The roof of the temple had long ago fallen through. There was, however, a small, cave-like opening at the rear of the sanctuary where the back of the original temple had rested against a low bluff of land.

Reaching the opening, I ducked to avoid bruising my head against the low archway. After feeling my way along three or four yards of a narrow passageway, the corridor opened into a large chamber. The space was dimly lit by a light source I could not detect. Then I noticed what appeared to be a white bed sheet on a large marble block near the doorway. It was as if someone knew I was coming. Chilled in my rain-soaked clothes, I quickly peeled them off and wrapped myself in the bed sheet. Feeling somewhat awkward in my new garment, I turned to make a closer examination of the chamber.

Directly opposite the entryway, and partially concealed by fallen ceiling and wall materials, was a heavy wooden door that looked like it came out of a Gothic novel. Despite its massiveness, it felt inviting rather than foreboding. I stepped across the room and tried to open it, but it was frozen shut. Alongside the door, poised as if to protect the threshold, was the life-sized statue of an ancient Greek god. Handsome and bearded, somehow I knew this image had been the holiest in the entire temple complex, and that the room in which I had taken shelter had originally been a hidden chamber in which occult initiations took place. Moving closer, I was drawn to the figure's eyes. Though cold and stony, they seemed to take on a life of their own, as if to invite my consciousness to step forward across an invisible threshold between my ordinary reality and the realm of the gods. In the flash of an instant, I found myself on the other side of the door, in an enormous cavern lit by thousands of candles. Hundreds of people, all wearing the same sheet-like garment, were seated in what appeared to be an ancient Greek theater absorbed in a lecture being delivered by a withered old man dressed in the garb of a Confucian scholar.

I sat down in the back of the stony auditorium and tried to listen, but it all sounded like gibberish to me — as if he was just repeating "ham and eggs, ham and eggs" over and over again. I turned to the person nearest me, a short fellow who reminded me of Yoda from Star Wars. *I asked him where I was and what the lecturer was saying. Yoda turned and faced me,*

gave me a stern look as if irritated that I had inter-
rupted his concentration, and said, "You were able to
get through the ten percent without a key, but you
forgot about the other ninety, you dork-head." And
then turned back to continue listening to the lecture.
Though he looked like Yoda, I knew it was John-
Roger.

Then a fellow sitting next to John-Roger, who was
wearing an aviator's cap from the early barnstorming
days, turned toward me and in a mocking voice said,
"You're half-baked Mr Eggo. You need to get
cooked." His appearance was as unfamiliar as the
Yoda character's, but I sensed he was John Morton.
John pulled out a huge, tarnished old key that looked
like the key to a horror movie dungeon, and, before I
had a chance to react, struck me over the head with
it. Startled by the abruptness of his action, I awoke to
find myself tangled up in a sheet in the familiar sur-
roundings of my own bedroom, still caught up in the
emotional reality of having been struck.

This vivid dream occurred a month or so after the dreamer had
begun to study with the Movement of Spiritual Inner
Awareness and marked a significant threshold in his understanding of the Movement. Unusually detailed (and, in its final
form, considerably embellished), this dream is otherwise typical of nocturnal experiences reported by MSIA participants.
Dreams, as I have already indicated in earlier chapters, are a
highly significant aspect of the MSIA "path."

The above experience was preceded by a period of confusion about MSIA, and the specific contents of the dream spoke
to the individual's puzzlement. A number of details — from
the academic lecture image to Yoda's remarks about 10% and

90% — have specialized meanings within MSIA, as reflected in the following passage from John-Roger's Dream Voyages:

> *The work of MSIA is about 10 percent on the physical level and about 90 percent on the spirit side, in the realms of Light. In the dream state, which reflects your activity in the other realms of Light, there are continuous seminars going on, continuous schooling, training, and learning. This training is going on all the time — "twenty-five hours a day, eight days a week." If you become aware of these levels, you can consciously receive more and more information from them. You have the potential for becoming more and more aware of them and using them as part of your daily living. When you are working directly with the Mystical Traveler, as a student preparing for initiation or as an initiate into the Sound Current, you will be involved in some experiences in the night travel that will be particular to that relationship.*

I have related the story of this dreamer's experience as a way of providing a vivid image for what it means to be a Movement participant on a day-to-day basis. What I see as central to understanding the MSIA path is the notion that participants are studying with a Mystery School — a spiritual school that, while having its roots in the ancient world (e.g., the Hellenistic mystery "schools") has been updated and adapted to the modern world. What I found attractive about the above dream, beyond its humor and wealth of detail, was the way in which it brought together the alternative (and, to my mind, more universal) image of treading the spiritual "path" (an image derived ultimately from pilgrimages) with the dominant Movement metaphor of attending a spiritual "school."

The dreamer begins by treading a path and then is "baptized" (a universal symbol for purification) by the rain. After divesting himself of his clothes — clothes can signify either one's old self, the physical body, or one's everyday persona — he makes a transition across a threshold to suddenly find himself in a seminar. Morton then initiates the seeker via the key he holds in his role as Mystical Traveler. The dreamer awakens and later finds that his puzzlement and confusion have dissipated — he can finally grasp the "teachings."

While I have already noted the importance of educational forms and images in the metaphysical/New Age subculture, it will repay our efforts if we develop this observation a little further before looking more closely at the experiences of individual Movement participants. Many of my remarks about the learning metaphor will refer to the larger metaphysical subculture and to the New Age movement — a movement from which MSIA consciously distances itself (as I have previously noted). Despite this distancing, the particular points I want to call attention to are shared by MSIA and the New Age.

Like other religious and cultural systems, the world view of the contemporary metaphysical subculture is held together by a shared set of symbols and metaphors — shared images of life reflected in the discourse of participants as a set of commonly used terms. For example, due partly to a vision of metaphysical unity inherited from theosophy and from Asian religious philosophy (but also due to this subculture's reaction against the perceived fragmentation and alienation of mainstream society), the metaphysical/New Age movement emphasizes the values of unity and relatedness. These values find expression in such common terms as "holistic," "oneness," "wholeness," and "community." This spiritual subculture also values growth and dynamism — an evaluation expressed in discourse about "evolution," "transformation," "process," and so forth.

If one reads New Age material long enough, one comes away overwhelmed by a sense of organic profusion.

The image of education is related to the growth metaphor (e.g., one of our linguistic conventions is that education allows a person to "grow"). If we examine the metaphysical subculture through the "lens" of the education theme, we discover that, in contrast to so many other religious movements, the dominant New Age/metaphysical "ceremonies" are workshops, lectures, and classes, rather than worship ceremonies. Even large New Age gatherings, such as the Whole Life Expo, resemble academic conferences more than they resemble camp meetings.

It is also interesting to note the extent to which educational metaphors inform New Age thought. In terms of the way the Western metaphysical tradition has interpreted the ongoing process of reincarnation, spiritual growth and even life itself are learning experiences. To cite some examples of this, Katar, a New Age medium who formerly resided in Santa Barbara, channels such messages as, "Here on Earth, you are your teacher, your books, your lessons, and the classroom as well as the student." This message is amplified by J.L. Simmons, a sociologist, who, in his *The Emerging New Age*, describes life on the physical plane as the "Earth School," and asserts that "We are here to learn . . . and will continue to return until we 'do the course' and 'graduate.'"

Similar images are reflected in an essay on "The Role of the Esoteric in Planetary Culture," where David Spangler argues that spiritual wisdom is esoteric "only because so few people expend the time, the energy, the effort, the openness, and the love to gain it, just as only a few are willing to invest what is required to become a nuclear physicist or a neurosurgeon." It would not be going too far to assert that, in the New Age vision of things, the image of the whole human life —

particularly when that life is directed toward spiritual goals —
can be summed up as a learning experience:

> *Each of us has an Inner Teacher, a part of ourselves*
> *which knows exactly what we need to learn, and con-*
> *stantly creates the opportunity for us to learn just*
> *that. We have the choice either to cooperate with this*
> *part of ourselves or to ignore it. If we decide to coop-*
> *erate, we can see lessons constantly in front of us;*
> *every challenge is a chance to grow and develop. If,*
> *on the other hand, we try to ignore this Inner*
> *Teacher, we can find ourselves hitting the same prob-*
> *lem again and again, because we are not perceiving*
> *and responding to the lesson we have created for our-*
> *selves. [It] is, however, the daily awareness of and*
> *cooperation with spirit [that] pulls humanity*
> *upwards on the evolutionary spiral, and the constant*
> *invocation and evocation of spirit enables a rapid*
> *unfolding of human potential. When the Inner*
> *Teacher and the evolutionary force of the Universe*
> *are able to work together with our full cooperation,*
> *wonders unfold.*
>
> *—From a 1986 flyer entitled*
> The Findhorn Foundation

In these passages, we see not only the decisive role of the
educational metaphor, but also how this metaphor has itself
been reshaped by the spiritual subculture's emphasis on holism
and growth. In other words, the kind of education this subculture values is the "education of the whole person," sometimes termed "holistic education," and this form of education
is an expression of the "evolutionary force of the Universe" (a
parallel to what, in more traditional language, might be called
the redemptive activity of the Holy Spirit). Thus, despite the

marked tendency to use images drawn from the sphere of formal education — a tendency that has created a realm of discourse saturated with metaphors of "classrooms," "graduations," and the like — the metaphysical subculture's sense of the educational process has tended to be more informal (more or less equivalent to learning in the most general sense), as well as more continuous — a process from which there may be periodic graduations, but from which there is never a FINAL GRADUATION after which the learning process ceases.

While some aspects of this view of the spiritual life as a learning experience are based on tradition (e.g., the Pythagorean "school"), the widespread appeal of this image of spirituality is the result of the manner in which modern society's emphasis on education informs our consciousness. The various social, economic, and historical forces that have led to the increased stress on education in the contemporary world are too complex to develop here. Obvious factors are such things as the increasing complexity of technology and of the socioeconomic system. Less obvious factors are such considerations as the need to delay the entry of new workers into the economic system. But whatever the forces at work in the larger society, by the time the baby boom generation began attending college in the 1960s, formal educational institutions had come to assume their present role as major socializing forces in Western societies. Being a college graduate and achieving higher, particularly professional degrees became associated with increased prestige and the potential for increased levels of income. In other words, to a greater extent than previously, education and educational accomplishments had become symbols of wealth and status.

Because the generation from which the majority of participants in the spiritual subculture has been recruited is the baby boom generation, the majority of participants in that subculture have been socialized to place a high value on education. Baby boomers, however, also tend to have been participants in the counterculture of the sixties, which means that they come from a generation that was highly critical of traditional, formal education.

While some members of that generation revolted against the educational establishment by denying the value of education altogether, other college students of the time reacted against what they saw as an irrelevant education by setting up alternative educational structures such as the so-called "free schools." These educational enterprises, which could offer students nothing in terms of degrees or certifications, were viable, at least for a time, because they offered courses on subjects people found intrinsically interesting — including such metaphysical topics as yoga, meditation, and so forth. The free school movement, in combination with the adult education programs that emerged in the seventies, provided the paradigms for the form many independent, metaphysical educational programs would eventually take.

Metaphysically-oriented groups like MSIA fit into the omnipresent educational ideology found in the contemporary spiritual subculture in at least two ways:

I. Firstly, such groups frequently (though not invariably) present their religious system via a wide variety of classes and workshops directed both to members and to the larger subculture. In some organizations — including MSIA — this educational outreach is a major activity, if not *the* major activity of the group. It should be noted, however, that even in such "classes," "seminars," and "workshops," much less stress is placed on a purely theoretical or intellectual knowledge than one would find in a mainstream educational setting. Rather, MSIA's teaching activities draw on both the free school tradition's emphasis on relevant and experiential education, and on the New Age movement's emphasis on learning that involves all levels of one's being ("holistic" education). As a consequence, MSIA classes tend to consist of about one-third information and about two-thirds interaction with others, sharing with the group, or some form of spiritual exercise.

II. Secondly, merely being a member of such a group is itself viewed as an educational experience. Thus becoming affiliated with an organization like MSIA is comparable to enrolling in a university ("joining a mystery school"), and the experiences one has in the Movement while participating in MSIA activities — as well as the experiences one encounters in one's life more generally — are viewed as part of one's course of study. In the words of one of the respondents to the MSIA survey:

> *MSIA is the most highly evolved and true "spiritual school" that I have ever seen, heard of, or read about. There are many beautiful religions out there, [but] I've found that no "teaching" can compare with one's personal experience of the light and love of the Holy Spirit, God, Christ, Traveler . . .*

It appears that many early Movement participants originally viewed the focus of their mystery school education as acquiring esoteric knowledge and experiences. For example, some of J-R's seminars, particularly the early seminars, dealt with such topics as the Lords of the Seven Rays, devic beings, details of the inner planes, and other subjects that constitute the bread-and-butter of theosophical and occult lectures. A passage from John-Roger's *Dream Voyages* — which, in context, is an aside to a larger discussion about meditating on a candle flame — is useful for illustrating this kind of discourse:

> *There is a devic force that works with the flame. It is a life force, a consciousness that is from the devic kingdom (which is the lower part of the angelic kingdom), and it is part of the fire's existence. Remember*

the Bible story of the prophet who was thrown into the furnace to burn? An angel appeared and protected him so that he was not harmed, even in the midst of the fire. This was a form of fire elemental or fire angel. They exist, and they have dominion over fire. They can control it and all its functions. There are people who are attuned to these fire forms and who can work with them. I've known people who could take burns away from the body because they worked with the fire lords. In ancient cultures, people almost always worshipped fire gods. In Hawaii, the god of the volcano was worshipped, which is a form of fire god. These forces definitely do exist, and communication with them can be established.

While plenty of this kind of information has been (and still is) presented in MSIA seminars, an examination of early Movement records reveals that — alongside of such esoteric data — John-Roger's teachings also stressed the importance of working out the flaws in one's psyche and learning to live everyday life as a sane, moral being. For example, in the very first issue of the first MSIA periodical, *On the Light Side,* one finds a J-R discourse that contains nonesoteric information about such straightforwardly psychological matters as how we displace our anger onto the people closest to us:

If you are full of tremendous inner turmoil and you're irritated, you are going to try to find somebody to blame for this irritation because you are not being responsible and controlling it and bringing it into balance. You will immediately shift it off onto the one nearest to you and that will probably be the person you love the most. And they often wonder, "How could you love me if you are treating me this

way and saying these things and doing this to me?"
The answer is, "I'm doing this to you because you're
the closest one around. An enemy would knock me
flat and my mother and father won't pay any atten-
tion but you're captive and I'm really going to let you
have it."

As the Movement matured, and, especially, as members of the Movement matured, the focus of many participants changed from acquiring exotic information about the inner planes to the more difficult and less glamorous task of hammering out one's impurities on the hard anvil of life. In line with this maturation process, the focus of the learning that is the essence of the MSIA path has gradually shifted from esoteric education to an emphasis on self-understanding and personal growth. And, while neither component has ever been completely eclipsed by the other, it is nevertheless clear to anyone who has observed and interacted with Movement participants (particularly in recent years) that learning about the self — as well as learning to be attentive to the promptings of the Light in one's everyday life — is central to the spiritual lives of most current MSIA members.

The learning that takes place in everyday life is conceptualized in a variety of ways. John-Roger teaches, for example, that one should "use everything for your growth," which refers, in particular, to the trials and challenges of everyday life. In one participant's words:

He [J-R] was giving pertinent information for all my
levels from the mundane paper work, to accepting
job responsibility, to having better emotional and
mental balance, and in my spiritual growth. I was
seeing answers to my questions. I had to have rea-
sons, and I found that I could take the information

John-Roger had given me and keep expanding it. There was always continuation and et cetera. Part of the teaching was to be able to use everything that happens; this is a fantastic key. If I was in a traffic jam, I could work on impatience. Or if I was required to do something that I didn't see any reason for, I could work on that area to make myself more complete. I started noticing things align in my daily life. I was taking on more responsibility.

Another way of understanding the challenges of everyday life is in terms of karma. *Karma*, as noted in an earlier chapter, is the moral equivalent of the law of cause and effect — roughly expressed in the familiar biblical idiom, "As one sows, so shall one reap." In terms of this idea, the problems and difficulties that confront one (as well as the positive things, though "good karma" is mentioned much less often than the unpleasant variety) are the direct results of the individual's past actions, either in this lifetime or in some past incarnation.

A widely assumed principle in the metaphysical subculture is that some conscious force or entity (a guardian angel, Lords of Karma, or some functional equivalent) is able to regulate the effects of one's karma so that each challenge provides the individual with a growth opportunity — a potential "learning experience," as it is often expressed. According to this line of thought, it is our own karma and not some external "devil" that is responsible for human suffering. Furthermore, it is the process of "learning the lessons" meted out by our karma that eventually empowers us to become liberated from the cycle of death and rebirth. As one respondent to the MSIA survey wrote:

My life has been a difficult one [and] I see the misery that people have all the time. I sometimes wonder

*how I and my mom and dad escaped from Nazi
Germany and certain death at the hands of the SS. . . .
If you believe in karma, then perhaps it can make
sense. If you believe we come back in reembodiment
to balance the scales and learn lessons, and that we
do this until we get it right, then it makes sense.*

As a core concept in this understanding of the "earth
school," karmic "lessons" have many facets. One way in
which karma teaches the (often reluctant) spiritual seeker is
through what has been termed "instant karma." While people
generally relate it to unpleasant experiences, it can also produce positive results:

*I was in the parking lot of a very crowded mall, and
had spotted a car pulling out of a space pretty close
to the mall entrance. Unfortunately, it was on the
other side of the lane from the way I was going. But
I was able to pull over and not block the traffic
behind me as I waited for the space. The person
pulling out was taking a lot of time, putting her pack-
ages away and stuff, and while I waited an expensive
car on the other side of the lane pulled into position
to take the soon-to-be-vacated space. I flashed my
lights at the "intruder" to signal I was already waiting for the space, and the person flashed their brights
back at me and jockeyed into closer position letting
me know in no uncertain terms they were claiming
the space despite my prior "rights" to it. At that
point I was faced with a choice: I could tough it out
and try to zip into the space when the car pulled out,
or I could just be calm about it, maintain my peace,
and let it go. I chose the latter, and as I moved along,*

another space, even closer to the mall opened up and I easily pulled in. "Now, this is instant karma," I thought. And as if to show me that there sometimes is "justice," as I walked into the mall, I glanced back and saw the expensive car still waiting for the space I had originally tried for.

A related form of karmic lesson is learning that one must give in order to receive:

When I first came to seminars people would come to me after it was over and exclaim, "Wasn't that seminar fantastic!" . . . [but] I didn't seem to be getting much out of it. I made up my mind to watch them during contributions to see what was happening, why they were so lifted, and why I was not. It was very interesting. They were giving of themselves. I had come to seminars to see what I could get out of them, never thinking that I had to give to get. Then, as every person spoke, I listened. If they were having problems, I would send them the Light, really being a part of them. I was giving of myself and sending the Light. The more I gave, the more I received. I would be bursting with the Light and I would want to hug everyone.

In addition to being a vehicle for our education, past karma is also viewed as posing an obstacle (a cosmic "debt") that must be surmounted ("repaid" in full) before we can proceed to the ultimate goal of Soul Transcendence. As a consequence, participants in MSIA conceptualize the challenges that confront them when they commit themselves to following the spiritual path as a "speeding up" of karma.

When I first started coming to seminars, [there were no] ups, no downs, pretty steady, and everything was going fine. But by my third seminar, everything had suddenly fallen apart . . . my entire world was down around my head. I could not understand it. I knew it was connected somehow with the seminars and with John-Roger, but I said in my contribution, "I don't know what is happening, John-Roger, but since I have been coming to seminars, everything has gone wrong. It's terrible!" Everyone laughed, and so did John-Roger. He said, "It looks as if you have been working off your karma prematurely — you are banging on the doors of Heaven wanting to get in, and things are coming down fast and heavy.

Another MSIA participant's account of how he was able to overcome frustration from a common everyday experience provides a useful example of how individuals treading the spiritual path learn from, and eventually overcome, difficult karma:

Sometimes it would take a couple of months to understand the teachings within my own level of consciousness. The Mystical Traveler Consciousness would bring the experience to me specifically for that teaching. For instance, somebody pulled into a parking place that I had just gone around the block to get after driving and looking for a half an hour. At first my expression was anger: "Why that dirty crumb! He got my place." Immediately after creating the emotions in my body, the teaching came in. I thought, "Oh yeah, last night at the seminar I was told about this type of situation. Because I understand that now, I don't have to do it anymore." But I had already done it. That was okay, because John-Roger didn't

*mind; he would bring me the experience again, a hun-
dred times if necessary. He was only interested in my
being able to clear these patterns. After a while the
frustration would start, and then the teaching would
come in before I went all the way through the action.
Later the teaching would come before the frustration
started. Once I had learned the lesson, people didn't
take my parking place anymore.*

As the spiritual advisor of the MSIA mystery school, John-
Roger embodies and exemplifies the goal of the school's educational process — he is someone who "knows" in a way that
simultaneously incorporates and yet transcends intellectual
knowledge. This sense of J-R as the Knower was expressed by
one of the respondents to the MSIA survey who first encountered John-Roger as a speaker at a metaphysical conference:

*The next day there was a question and answer session
with several of the speakers. John-Roger blew all of
the other guys away. He just seemed to know the
answers. It wasn't a theory, it wasn't a belief system,
it wasn't a nice thought — he just knew. And I kept
thinking, "He knows. This guy knows."*

In addition to his generic teachings, John-Roger has sometimes
(particularly in the early days) focused his educating activity
on individual students. This aspect of his work with aspirants
can take many forms. In one case recorded in an early
Movement publication, *Across the Golden Bridge*, John-Roger
suggested a "homework" exercise that addressed someone's
specific personal issue:

*One personality trait that came out of my Light
Study was my feeling of being cut off and alone in a
group. [John-Roger] said that I could break through*

this pattern by introducing myself to fifty people. "Hi, my name is John. How are you?" I decided it was a good idea and started at a supermarket in Newport Beach, California, but I only introduced myself to a couple of people. Next I did it in Isla Vista, a UCSB student community. This time I introduced myself to about thirty people, although I would skip those who looked unfriendly. Finally, one day between classes I started from the middle of campus and even though I was scared, worked my way toward the edge, determined not to miss anyone. I stopped long enough to establish contact, and then went on to the next person. By the time I had gotten through fifty, I was ready to keep going. I broke through the pattern, which helped me to feel closer to people.

For most of the people who have worked with and assisted John-Roger personally, and for some of the people who have had fairly extensive personal contact with him, J-R has sometimes resorted to unorthodox teaching tactics that these students have found extremely disconcerting. For example, one long-term Movement participant related the following incident during an interview:

I was driving in a car with J-R. He turned to me and said, "By the way, don't ever trust David Gold" [another Movement participant; not his real name]. Immediately when he said that, I felt a lurch inside. And I said, "Oh really, Why?" He says, "Well, you never know" — some vague thing. I felt repulsed. . . . and then, to my sheer disgust, I said, "I know what you mean J-R." I had no clue what he meant. I was so busy brown-nosing, and wanting to be accepted by him, and to be a part of the inner circle, that I left my own truth and moved into this brown-nosing consciousness. J-R looked at me, and then looked out the window, and didn't say another word to me. I felt like dirt and I was close to hating him. I was so angry.

It took me about three months [of confusion and inner conflict] before it finally dawned on me: If J-R had turned to me and said, "Sita [not her real name], you persist in brown-nosing me. You persist in letting go of what you know is the truth in your own heart. You so much want to be accepted by others that you enter into illusions you know are not real and become a part of them. You lie and you underestimate yourself and you belittle yourself and you belittle the truth that's in your own heart." [If he'd confronted me directly,] I would have immediately gone into self-protection, given all sorts of explanation of why not, and I couldn't have gotten the teaching. So what he did was to manifest the ugly little demon. Then, when I finally picked it up, . . . it was one of the most profound teachings of my life.

This interviewee felt that the kind of challenging teaching style exemplified in this experience with John-Roger — which, on the face of it, seems harsh and even cruel — explains, at least partially, the many negative stories that disgruntled former staff members have related about J-R.

Another arena in which individualized learning experiences are possible is during certain altered states of consciousness, such as during dream states.

In contrast with many other metaphysical groups, dreams are a highly significant part of the MSIA path. As one might anticipate, educational images have been extended to encompass and interpret such states. Thus, as John-Roger asserts in the passage cited earlier in the present chapter, in the dream state there are "continuous seminars going on, continuous schooling, training, and learning." In the dream realm, dreamers enter "halls of learning" in which they can attend lectures on metaphysical subjects, as we saw with the dreamer who reported listening to the discourse of a Confucian scholar.

The notion of halls of learning or halls of wisdom that one attends in the hours of sleep is actually quite widespread in the metaphysical subculture, particularly in the theosophical tradition, though the idea is rarely developed at length. The work of theosophical author Alice A. Bailey may be taken as typical in this regard. In several of her books, Bailey describes the halls of learning in the following way:

> *Classes are held . . . in the Hall of Learning and the method is much the same as in the big universities — classes at certain hours, experimental work, examinations, and a gradual moving up and onward as the tests are passed. . . . In the Hall of Learning the pupil is taught nightly for a short time before proceeding with any work of service. This teaching he brings over into his physical brain consciousness in the form of a deep interest in certain subjects. . . . [Such experiences may also be reflected in] dreams which are symbolic presentations of teaching received in the hours of sleep by aspirants and disciples in the Hall of Learning on the highest level of the astral plane, and in the Hall of Wisdom on the mental plane.*

Attending night school in the halls of learning does not automatically mean that dreamers will consciously remember their nocturnal experiences upon awakening. In fact, most do not remember. As John-Roger notes:

> *You will wake up knowing that you were taught something during the night. You'll know you were in*

a class. Most often, if you've been on the mental plane, you may not see people or remember particular places. Your memory will probably be more related to ideas, knowledge, and thoughts; it will be a mental process. You may remember hearing part of a lecture or someone reading out of a book, but you may not be able to remember anything of the lesson.

One's failure to remember dream learning does not obviate its significance, as the discussion in Chapter One indicated. Because MSIA is the exoteric expression of a specific esoteric school, participants sometimes report sharing the same dream landscape with other participants — as if a group of MSIA members met together during "night school":

I've had many dreams in which John-Roger played a starring role. I would tell someone about a dream, and they'd begin to tell me about the same dream. We would find out that there were three or four people in on the dream, and that it was an actual experience on the other side in which we were all gathered.

While such group dreams are not uncommon, the great majority of learning dreams remembered by Movement participants embody individualized lessons, often with John-Roger. The following experience is typical in this regard:

[In my dream] you [John-Roger] challenged me to do some interesting things like sitting cross-legged upside down on the ceiling. My fear blocked me. You explained to me that the trick to it was in my perception of the space. . . . It is interesting that the key seems to be one of perception rather than of trying harder.

Significant spiritual dreams need not, of course, always involve J-R, nor need they necessarily be dreams in which one explicitly learns something. The following dream, for instance, was described to me by one longtime Movement participant:

> *I'd never thought once about doing ordinations — it had not even crossed my mind. One night, during which I had slept only three hours, I was shown how to do ordinations. So I woke up, and, when I remembered it, my first thought was, "Oh no, please." I'm already stretching myself to facilitate [MSIA events]. But I said [to myself], I have got to write and ask if this is really how one does this, and the reply came back, "Yes." So what happens to me a lot now is that, if I pay attention, I'm shown things on the other side that are coming forward. But that's begun to happen only after years and years and years of wanting to discern what's the truth and what's karma and all that.*

This dream seemed to be directing this individual to undertake a particular kind of service work. Soon afterwards, she became involved in the ordaining of MSIA ministers.

One of the more unusual aspects of John-Roger's teachings on the significance of the dream state is the notion that individuals can experience and overcome a certain amount of one's negative karma in dreams. This is a notion which, if not unique to MSIA, is an idea that I have never come across anywhere else. It explains, among other phenomena, certain kinds of nightmares:

> *There is a master force, or dream master, from the spiritual realms who works with the students of MSIA. One of the reasons the dream state becomes*

so valuable spiritually is because, through the action of this dream master, you are allowed to balance actions in the dream state instead of on the physical level. How would you like to live through those nightmares in an awake state? Through this special action, many negative actions (like car wrecks, accidents, or other dangerous or threatening situations, etc.) have been bypassed in the physical and completed on another realm through the dream process.

Like everyday life, dreams can also provide situations in which the aspirant can learn from one's karma through working on one's responses to trying situations. Compare, for instance, the following dream experience with the experience of the person who was angered by other people always taking his parking place:

I had a dream where there was a woman in trouble, and she was talking to me on the telephone; she was in dire, desperate straits, suffering, and needed help immediately. There were many people around me cutting up, making noise, making fun, and pulling the telephone away. I got extremely angry and infuriated. In my earlier dreams I had lashed back at these people. But this time I was at the point where I just took a book and threw it against the wall. I wouldn't unleash it against somebody, but I still had it there to unleash. I woke up in a sweat, and said, "No, no, I blew it. I want to go back and do it right."

The implication in this passage, which is taken from *Across the Golden Bridge*, is that this individual was having a dream experience in which he was gradually improving how he reacted to an irritating experience he was encountering over and over again in a series of dreams. The parallel with the other individual's reactions to his "parking place karma" is quite close, indicating a greater or lesser degree of interchangeability between learning in the dream state and learning in the waking state.

But what, we might well ask ourselves at this point, is the goal of such learning? Why bother to invest so much effort into changing our personality patterns? Is it really so bad to just react to life spontaneously? Should we really be trying to radically modify ordinary human nature? While such questions invite more than one response, it might be most meaningful if we focused on the question of naturalness.

"Natural" means to be in accord with the nature of a thing. In most religious traditions, a human being is viewed as having more than one "nature." The deepest and most real part of ourselves — the soul or higher self — has, in the traditional view, a Christ-like nature that transcends the pettiness of our everyday life. From this perspective, the day-to-day struggles with the less pleasant aspects of our personality is really an effort to heal the split between our two natures by bringing our everyday personality into alignment with our soul. Or, in a somewhat different religious idiom, one might say that the goal is to learn to surrender ourselves to God. In the words of one Movement participant:

> *I seem to be the most relaxed and at my best when [I can say], "Okay God, I'm yours. It's your breath, it's your body, it's your heart, it's your mind. Use me. Guide me. Show me." I hope I'm a good listener. I do my best to follow and to live my life that way. And that's really where I'm going. I want to be a freed up vessel to hold God's consciousness.*

"Prana" — the MSIA headquarters in Los Angeles, CA.

John-Roger circa 1974.

John-Roger working on correspondence, mid 1970s.

John-Roger in the early 1970s.

John-Roger at an annual conference in Los Angeles, CA.

John-Roger at an Insight graduation ceremony, circa 1981.

John-Roger visiting the MSIA community in Nigeria.

John-Roger on his travels around the world.

John-Roger meditating atop the Great Pyramid at Giza.

John-Roger visiting a new friend at Windermere Ranch in
Santa Barbara, CA.

John-Roger in 1996.

John-Roger co-facilitating an MSIA workshop with
John Morton.

John-Roger and John Morton having some fun at a retreat.

John Morton in the earlier days.

John Morton running with the Olympic torch for the
Los Angeles Games in 1984.

John Morton with the Olympic torch in 1984.

Laura Donnelley-Morton and John Morton at a fund-raising event.

John Morton at the Great Pyramid in 1995.

John Morton at Windermere Ranch in Santa Barbara.

John Morton in 1996.

7

DEMOGRAPHIC PROFILES OF MEMBERS AND EX-MEMBERS

Following the model of biology, sociologists of religion have from time to time attempted to delineate systems for classifying religious organizations according to their social structure and according to their relationship with the larger society. One of the most commonly used typologies applied to North American religious bodies is the cult-sect-denomination schema. In terms of this schema, "sect" is most often used to designate a group that schisms off from a larger denomination, often in the name of reforming and purifying the tradition. Unlike denominations, which, for the most part, coexist peacefully with the social mainstream, sects tend to take a stance of antagonism toward certain elements of the society. This conflict can range from relatively mild, such as refusing to watch box office movies or refusing to wear make-up, to more radical kinds of distancing, such as refusing to serve in the military or refusing to send one's children to public schools.

The discussion in J. Milton Yinger's, *Religion, Society, and the Individual,* constitutes the starting point for all subsequent sociological discussions of schemas of religious classification. In this work, Yinger included a discussion of what he called "established sects," namely religious reform movements that, once they settled into society and into the routines of their own organizational life, retain certain sectarian characteristics while simultaneously achieving stability and persisting across several generations (e.g., the Quakers and the Latter-Day Saints Church). In North America, the word "sect" does not have particularly negative connotations. This is in sharp contrast to Europe, where sect is a highly pejorative designation, not unlike the term "cult" in the North American setting. "Cult" has several, related meanings. In sociological circles prior to the cult controversy of the 1970s, "cult" was a value-neutral term referring to small, informal religious groups, particularly transitory groups in the metaphysical-occult subculture that gathered around charismatic religious leaders. Many new religions, from Christianity to MSIA, originated as "cults" in the technical sense of that term.

Beyond their informality, cults are characterized as having mystical, esoteric doctrines. As a result of this esoteric orientation, cults tend not to be interested in making this world a better place in which to live, neither are they usually interested in entering into dialogue with other religions. They also typically appeal to only one age group and to only one economic class. For different reasons, sects tend to exhibit these same traits (otherworldly and nondialogue oriented) and the same kind of narrow demographic profile.

By the middle of the 1970s, "cult" had become a pejorative term, applied to any unpopular religious group. Because of its pejorative connotations, mainstream scholars working in the field now tend to avoid the term, preferring the label "new religion" or "new religious movement." It should also be noted that the groups that came to occupy center stage during the cult controversy of the mid-seventies had both cult-like characteristics (e.g., mystical doctrines) and sect-like characteristics (e.g., strict boundaries), making the older cult-sect distinction less applicable to many of the more recent new religions.

For a variety of reasons, sectarian religions — religions which, at the time of their founding, tend to set themselves apart from the surrounding culture — gradually accommodate themselves to society until they become mainstream denominations. H. Richard Neibuhr examined this dynamic process in his classic work, *The Social Sources of Denominationalism*. As one might anticipate, contemporary new religions are going through a similar transformation, in the sense that they are becoming progressively more denominational in their organizational and demographic profiles.

The present chapter reports demographic data on the Church of the Movement of Spiritual Inner Awareness from two sources. The first source is MSIA's internal statistical report on Discourse subscribers for September 1995. I was informed that these figures fluctuate from month to month, so that the monthly report represents a "snapshot" of a dynamic and constantly changing population. The second source is a survey mailed to a sampling of current and former members of the Movement of Spiritual Inner Awareness in early 1995. In the interests of simplicity, I restricted the sample to U.S. residents, feeling that MSIA's internal report would provide adequate data for non-U.S. residents. For current members, this was accomplished by mailing a simple, one-page questionnaire to a random sample of 800 current U.S. Discourse subscribers. Being "on Discourses," as subscribing to MSIA's monthly lessons is referred to by members, is the basic criterion for identifying people who are actively involved in the Movement.

I had hoped that enough people would respond to produce 150–200 completed surveys and had counted on the goodwill of members to give me a high enough return rate that we would not have to undertake a second mailing. I was totally unprepared to receive 447 questionnaires — a return rate of 56%! This must break some kind of record for surveys of this type.

While the return rate for Discourse subscribers surprised me, the return rate for ex-members amazed me. A two-page survey — containing the same items as the current member questionnaire plus an extra page to measure postinvolvement attitudes — was mailed to 200 former subscribers. As a random sample that incorporated people who had dropped out years prior to the mailing, I anticipated that many of the addresses would be out of date. I also wondered how many people would bother to fill out a rather boring form about a group in which they were no longer active. In my wildest dreams, I did not expect to receive more than 20 to 25 ex-member questionnaires. Instead, I was sent 53, representing a return rate of 26.5%.

These two subsamples, current and former Discourse subscribers, were comparable in many ways. Thus in the following discussion of the survey's findings, I will collapse the statistics from current members and ex-members on items where the differences between the two subsamples are statistically insignificant. Where the differences are significant, the sample will be split and the differences discussed.

Sex Ratio and Total Membership

Examining MSIA's internal statistical report for September 1995, I found almost twice as many female (3,003) as opposed to male (1,605) Discourse subscribers. This accords well with informal observations of attendees at MSIA events, which always attract a marked predominance of women. The attribution of sex was based upon subscribers' first names. Because the sex of certain names could not be determined (particularly for African subscribers), I could not classify 232 members of the population. This adds up to a total of 4,840 active subscribers.

There are, however, large numbers of people whose subscriptions lapse for shorter or longer periods of time who later reactivate their subscriptions. MSIA's computer system quickly moves people into the "Lapsed" category whenever they forget to send in their yearly Discourse pledge of $100, which can be waived if someone cannot afford it. "Lapsed" members have been active some time within the preceding 17 months. After this time span has elapsed, they are reclassified as "Inactive." Because many "Lapsed" individuals eventually renew their subscriptions, a significant percentage should still be regarded as members. MSIA's September report notes a total of 1,897 "Lapsed." An accurate estimate of the group's membership would probably fall somewhere between five and six thousand.

International Distribution

As one would anticipate, the largest number of Discourse subscribers reside inside the United States. In September of 1995, active U.S. subscribers totaled 2,644. Of these, 48 were taking Spanish-language Discourses. In the same month, MSIA's internal report shows a total of 2,162 (close to half) of all Discourse subscribers residing outside the U.S. By language, non-U.S. Discourses totaled 1,065 English, 1,071 Spanish, and 26 French.

The organization has invested a great deal of energy into translating its various materials into Spanish, as many current MSIA members reside in Latin America and almost a hundred live in Spain. At the time of this study, only the first few years of Discourses had been translated into French. A beginning had also been made translating the Discourses into Japanese, but this task was never completed beyond the first couple of lessons. The same holds true for translating them into German.

The worldwide distribution of Discourses in September of 1995 was 403 in Australia (10 in New Zealand), 277 in Western Europe (97 Spanish-language and 26 French-language), 383 in Africa, 870 in South America, 2798 in North America (61 in Canada and 93 Spanish-language in Mexico), and 88 in other areas of the world. The great majority (101) of English-language subscribers in Europe resides, as one would antici-pate, in England. Sweden was the second largest European consumer of English-language Discourses, with 17 subscribers. South American subscribers were confined to five countries: Colombia (304), Argentina (203), Chile (191), Uruguay (90), and Venezuela (82). Of the 383 Discourse subscribers in Africa, the vast majority lives in Nigeria, with fewer than one dozen living in other African countries (e.g., Ghana and South Africa). The balance of the present chapter will examine data from the questionnaire mailed to U.S. residents.

Age

Charting age by decade of birth gives us a straightforward pat-tern in which the birthdays of almost three-fourths of the sur-vey respondents fall within the baby boomer decades of the 1940s and the 1950s, and another fifth of the respondents in either the 1930s or the 1960s (Table 7.1). This finding corre-sponds with the impressionistic sense one has when attending MSIA events that the bulk of participants are baby-boomers, with a more-than-token smattering of older and young-er members.

Thus, membership is simultaneously concentrated in the baby boom generation and yet distributed across all age categories. In the traditional sociological discussion of cults, sects, and denominations, cults tend to draw from a single age group, and denominations tend to draw from several generations. The age profile of MSIA members reflected in this survey places it somewhere between a denomination and a cult. (The technical, sociological category of cult should be carefully distinguished from the popular, pejorative use of this term.) My sense is that as MSIA moves into the future, the age distribution will continue to shift toward a denominational profile. It should be noted that Discourses are written for adults. Thus, 1980 was the latest birthday year of Discourse subscribers surveyed.

Table 7.1 — Decade of Birth

Decade	Count	Percentage
1900–09	1	0.2
1910–19	8	1.6
1920–29	20	4.0
1930–39	51	10.2
1940–49	187	37.4
1950–59	185	37.0
1960–69	44	8.8
1970–80	2	0.4
No response	2	0.4
TOTAL	500	100.0

Nation of Birth

Because the questionnaire was sent only to U.S. residents, over 90% of respondents reported being born in the United States (Table 7.2). This statistic would have been significantly different, of course, had the sample been compiled from both U.S. and non-U.S. residents. Much of MSIA's recent growth has come from Mexico and South America, so that a significant number of members are now Latin American.

Table 7.2 — Birthplace

Country	Count	Percent
U.S.	461	92.2
Non-U.S.	36	7.2
No response	3	0.6
TOTAL	500	100.0

Citizenship

Given the nature of the sample, it was not surprising to find that over 95% of respondents were United States citizens (Table 7.3).

Table 7.3 — Citizenship

Country	Count	Percent
U.S.	484	96.8
Non-U.S.	15	3.0
No response	1	0.2
TOTAL	500	100.0

Area of Residence

Respondents were also asked in which area of the country they currently resided. Consistent with expectations, because MSIA began and is still headquartered in Los Angeles, the largest subgrouping — almost 40% — resided in California. The second largest subgroup resided in the Northeast, and the third largest in the Southwest (Table 7.4).

Table 7.4 — Area of Residence

Area	Count	Percent
California	194	38.8
Northeast	100	20.0
Southwest	64	12.8
Northwest	36	7.2
Southeast	31	6.2
Plains	25	5.0
Florida	23	4.6
Non-U.S.	15	3.0
Alaska-Hawaii	7	1.4
No response	5	1.0
TOTAL	500	100.0

Marital Status

Marital status is one of the statistics for which there was a significant difference between current and ex-members of MSIA. Almost half (47%) of all Discourse subscribers are presently married in contrast to less than a third (28%) of all former subscribers (Tables 7.5 and 7.6).

Table 7.5 — Currently Involved: Marital Status

Status	Count	Percent
Single	102	22.8
Married	210	47.0
Divorced/Separated	127	28.4
Widow	6	1.3
No response	2	0.4
TOTAL	447	100.0

Table 7.6 — Formerly Involved: Marital Status

Status	Count	Percent
Single	18	34.0
Married	15	28.3
Divorced/Separated	19	35.8
Widow	1	1.9
TOTAL	53	100.0

What does this difference between the two subsamples indicate? Because there is no significant difference age-wise, the difference in percentage of single people cannot be explained away as a function of age. Another hypothesis might be that the greater number of divorced respondents among ex-members can be explained in terms of marital disputes resulting from the exit of one spouse from MSIA while the other spouse remained. This hypothesis was, however, not substantiated by answers on the questionnaires, which requested former members to describe their leaving MSIA. Furthermore, this type of explanation fails to explain the larger percentage of people who had never been married in the ex-member sub-sample.

This leaves two alternatives: Either (1) the kind of person who sticks with a commitment to a religious group also tends to be the kind of person who can commit to a marriage, or (2) there is something about belonging to MSIA that promotes and/or reinforces the married state. Initially, I favored the first explanation. MSIA's teachings, while not unfavorable toward marriage, simultaneously do not exalt the married state as an ideal. Also, John-Roger's status as a person who has never been married does not provide a model for married life, although John Morton, the spiritual director of MSIA and the current Mystical Traveler, has been married since 1990.

However, as I became more familiar with MSIA's teachings, I realized that J-R has consistently taught that difficulties — including marital difficulties — should be regarded as opportunities for growth rather than as evils to be escaped. MSIA also teaches that it is important to take responsibility for one's own life, rather than blaming circumstances or other people. Discourse subscribers are regularly brought into contact with this type of thinking through their monthly Discourses, if not through MSIA tapes, lectures, and other readings. Thus, serious members trying to put what they are being taught into action would be prompted to keep working on their marriages in ways that nonmembers might not. As a consequence, it now appears to me that this second explanation is at least as significant — if not more so — for understanding the correlation between membership and marriage as the first explanation.

Children

Given the larger number of married people among current Discourse subscribers, I was surprised to find no statistically significant difference in number of children between current and ex-members. The pattern for both subsamples was almost exactly the same (Table 7.7).

Table 7.7 — Number of Children

Number	Count	Percent
None	227	45.4
1 Child	89	17.8
2 Children	115	23.0
3 or More	68	13.6
No Response	1	0.2
TOTAL	500	100.0

Once again, there is nothing in MSIA's teachings that would particularly encourage or discourage a couple from having children, since this, like marriage, is an area of life on the physical ("10 %") level, and J-R teaches that each person needs to decide about these things for himself/herself. So why should there be more couples in MSIA having fewer children per marriage than among former members? My tentative hypothesis is that MSIA members' fewer-children-per-marriage is a result of the greater percentage of business and professional people (see discussion of Table 7.10 below) who are more likely to prioritize their careers over raising a family.

Education

Another point on which the two subsamples differed was education. Specifically, a significantly higher percentage of current Discourse subscribers had completed a master's degree than former subscribers. The ex-member subsample compensated for its lower percentage of master's degrees by a correspondingly higher number of respondents who had attended college but who had not received a bachelor's degree (Tables 7.8 and 7.9).

Table 7.8 — Currently Involved: Highest Degree

Schooling	Count	Percent
High School	49	11.0
Some College	60	13.4
Bachelor's	146	32.7
Master's	166	37.1
Ph.D.	21	4.7
Other	2	0.4
No Response	3	0.7
TOTAL	447	100.0

Table 7.9 — Formerly Involved: Highest Degree

Schooling	Count	Percent
High School	5	9.4
Some College	11	20.8
Bachelor's	18	34.0
Master's	14	26.4
Ph.D.	4	7.5
No Response	3	0.7
TOTAL	53	100.0

A significant factor shaping this educational pattern is that over a decade ago John-Roger helped to give birth to the University of Santa Monica (USM), a graduate school offering master's degrees in psychology. Particularly in the early years of its institutional life, MSIA members were the mainstay of USM because it offered an approach to education they found unique and valuable — and which subsequently proved so to the educational community at large. As a consequence, a number of current members hold USM master's degrees.

Occupation

In the United States, the most important factor determining class status is one's occupation. On this item, there was once again a significant difference between current and former members, with more current members pursuing higher-status careers than ex-members (Tables 7.10 and 7.11).

Table 7.10 — Currently Involved: Occupation

Occupation	Count	Percent
Professional	100	22.4
Business, Manager	92	20.6
Technical, Skilled	64	14.3
Teacher, Research	40	8.9
Artist	32	7.2
Clerical, Manual	59	13.2
Unemp, Stud, Home, Ret.	56	12.5
No Response	4	0.9
TOTAL	447	100.0

Table 7.11 — Formerly Involved: Occupation

Occupation	Count	Percent
Professional	9	17.0
Business, Manager	8	15.1
Technical, Skilled	8	15.1
Teacher, Research	3	5.7
Artist	5	9.4
Clerical, Manual	10	18.9
Unemp, Stud, Home, Ret.	10	18.9
TOTAL	53	100.0

Income

The difference in occupation was, unsurprisingly, reflected as a difference in income between current and former MSIA Discourse subscribers (Tables 7.12 and 7.13).

Table 7.12 — Currently Involved: Income

Yearly Income	Count	Percent
< $10,000	26	5.8
10–20,000	43	9.6
20–40,000	138	30.9
40–60,000	105	23.5
60–100,000	59	13.2
> 100,000	39	8.7
No Response	37	8.3
TOTAL	447	100.0

Table 7.13 — Formerly Involved: Income

Yearly Income	Count	Percent
< $10,000	5	9.4
10–20,000	11	20.8
20–40,000	14	26.4
40–60,000	10	18.9
60–100,000	2	3.8
>100,000	6	11.3
No Response	5	9.4
TOTAL	53	100.0

MSIA's occupational and income patterns indicate a membership that has been comparatively successful in our society's economic arena. These findings fly in the face of the popular stereotype of cults — a stereotype that portrays members of minority religions as financially exploited drones who toil long hours at demeaning, low-skill jobs for the sole purpose of enlarging the leader's bank account.

The income differences between current and former members indicate either (1) that as a group, ex-member respondents had less financial potential to begin with, or (2) that remaining a member of MSIA tends to promote financial success. Like the marriage item, my first inclination for this item was to attribute the difference to the different personal tendencies of respondents. In other words, the same personality type that strives for economic success also tends to stay with their chosen spiritual path, and vice versa.

However, MSIA also encourages members to cultivate an attitude that attracts abundance. Although John-Roger's teachings on wealth are placed in a larger context of well-being (e.g., as presented in the books *Wealth and Higher*

Consciousness and *Wealth 101*), they nevertheless encourage members to seek a state of healthy prosperity. People who remain in MSIA are regularly brought into contact with J-R's low-key prosperity teachings through tapes, lectures, and other readings, and they would thus be encouraged to become financially successful. As a consequence, it now appears to me that this influence is at least as significant for understanding the correlation between membership and career success as one's personality type.

Political Affiliation

Despite the economic differences between current and former Discourse subscribers, there was no significant difference between the pattern of their political affiliation, which was overwhelmingly (45.8%) Democratic (Table 7.14).

Table 7.14 — Political Party

Affiliation	Count	Percent
Republican	72	14.4
Democratic	229	45.8
Independent	53	10.6
Other	14	2.8
Nonpolitical	82	16.4
No Response	50	10.0
TOTAL	500	100.0

What little difference there was between current and former members pointed to exactly the opposite of what one might expect, given that economic success tends to be correlated with affiliation with the Republican Party. Specifically,

14.3% of current members are Republicans and 45.9% Democrats, in contrast to ex-members who are 15.1% Republicans and 45.3% Democrats.

While the generally liberal political orientation of MSIA members is not a surprising finding, it contrasts sharply with the conservative political inclinations of certain other, comparable minority religions. The Unification Church and the Church Universal and Triumphant, for example, are socially conservative, and the great majority of their members are Republicans.

Race

There was no significant difference between current and former Discourse subscribers on race. Consistent with previous research on new religions, the overwhelming majority of MSIA members in the United States are non-Hispanic Caucasians (Table 7.15). Clearly this statistic would have been different had non-U.S. members been surveyed. For example, of the 383 African Discourse subscribers, all but a dozen or so live in Nigeria and are black.

Table 7.15 — Race

Heritage	Count	Percent
Caucasian	460	92.0
Black	5	1.0
Asian	2	0.4
Hispanic	13	2.6
Native American	3	0.6
No Response	17	3.4
TOTAL	500	100.0

The lack of a statistically significant difference between current and former members on this item indicates, among other things, that the economic differences between the two subsamples is not a function of respondents' race.

Religious Heritage

Yet another item on which there was no significant difference between current and ex-members was the religious tradition in which they were raised. Consistent with previous research on new religions, a disproportionate number — when compared with the general population — of MSIA respondents were from Jewish households (14%), though many families were clearly nonpracticing Jews. Also consistent with previous research, a disproportionate number of respondents were raised Catholic (27%), though the departure of this statistic from the general population was comparatively slight (Table 7.16). Clearly, the proportion of people from Catholic backgrounds would have been substantially larger had Latin American and Spanish members been surveyed.

Table 7.16 — Religious Heritage

Heritage	Count	Percent
Jewish	71	14.2
Catholic	135	27.0
Protestant	256	51.2
Other	12	2.4
None	23	4.6
No Response	3	0.6
TOTAL	500	100.0

In addition to religious heritage, the questionnaire also requested respondents to mention any other religious group with which they had been affiliated prior to joining MSIA. Although over 90% of respondents were brought up in traditional faiths, almost half of the respondents had been affiliated with one or more nontraditional religious groups after their childhood affiliation and prior to their membership in the Movement of Spiritual Inner Awareness. Groups mentioned by respondents ranged widely from metaphysical churches to Hindu yoga groups. This evidence of multiple memberships after childhood indicates a "seeker" mentality and a demonstrable quest for spiritual meaning before joining the Movement of Spiritual Inner Awareness.

Length of Membership

The questionnaire contained a number of items designed to measure the length and depth of respondents' membership. As one might anticipate, there were significant differences between current and former members on these items. The simplest measure was years of membership (Tables 7.17 and 7.18).

Table 7.17 — Currently Involved: Years of Membership

Years	Count	Percent
0–5 years	94	21.0
6–10 years	103	23.0
11–15 years	87	19.5
16–20 years	79	17.7
21–25 years	76	17.0
No Response	8	1.8
TOTAL	447	100.0

Table 7.18 — Formerly Involved: Years of Membership

Years	Count	Percent
0–5 years	25	47.2
6–10 years	13	24.5
11–15 years	3	5.7
16–20 years	7	13.2
21–25 years	1	1.9
No Response	4	7.5
TOTAL	53	100.0

While I was not surprised to find substantially shorter membership periods for ex-members, I did not expect to find that over half of those who had left MSIA did so after being involved for more than five years. Previous longitudinal studies, such as Saul Levine's work (reported in his book *Radical Departures*), have indicated that more than 90% of those who join an intensive religious group drop out after only two years or less of membership.

I believe that this unanticipated finding can best be explained in terms of the contrast between the nature of participation in MSIA and participation in most of the groups studied by Levine. Unlike such "high-demand" groups as the Hare Krishnas, membership in MSIA does not involve leaving mainstream society and taking up residence in a new, highly defined world strictly segregated from the mainstream. While one may participate in a wide range of MSIA activities that can, if one so desires, fill up most of one's free time, one may also simply read Discourses and practice one's spiritual exercises and still be regarded as a member in good standing. In other words, MSIA is not a high-demand group in the same sense as Levine's sample of movements were high-demand groups.

Another unanticipated finding was that the current membership had joined the Movement of Spiritual Inner Awareness at a wide variety of different times over the past twenty-five years, as the more or less even distribution of respondents within each five-year period indicates. Based on the predominance of baby boomers, I had expected that a larger number of members would have entered the Movement during the seventies. Once again, had a significant number of questionnaires been sent to nonresidents of the United States, I believe I would have seen a higher number of respondents in the more recent five-year intervals because of MSIA's relatively recent growth in Latin American countries.

Level of Initiation

Beyond simply the number of years one has spent in MSIA, there are other criteria for determining the depth of one's involvement. Chief among these is level of initiation attained. As indicated in earlier chapters, there are four formal initiations. Sequentially, these are the causal, mental, etheric, and soul initiations. As their longer involvement would lead one to expect, proportionally more current members had received the higher initiations than former members (Tables 7.19 and 7.20).

Table 7.19 — Currently Involved: Highest Initiation

Initiation	Count	Percent
Non-Initiate	54	12.1
Causal	65	14.5
Mental	47	10.5
Etheric	110	24.6
Soul	127	28.4
No Response	44	9.8
TOTAL	447	100.0

Table 7.20 — Formerly Involved: Highest Initiation

Initiation	Count	Percent
Non-Initiate	19	35.8
Causal	12	22.6
Mental	4	7.5
Etheric	8	15.1
Soul	4	7.5
No Response	6	11.3
TOTAL	53	100.0

Another statistic indicating depth of involvement is whether one chooses to become an MSIA minister. Ordination in MSIA is seen as a spiritual calling and is not tied to formal academic training. Members can apply to become ordained after two years of study and after having received the causal (first) initiation. Given this, it is comparatively easy for even relatively new members to become ministers, and a large percentage of currently involved respondents (almost two-thirds: 66.4%) are ministers. By way of contrast, less than a third (32.1%) of ex-members had been MSIA ministers.

MSIA's internal report for September 1995 notes 2,550 active ministers worldwide, with 1,644 in the U.S. — about 62% of the U.S. population of active subscribers. The difference between this figure and the 66.4% reported in the survey probably reflects the higher motivation of respondents, more of whom would be ministers, as opposed to nonordained Discourse subscribers who received the survey but who did not respond.

Affiliation

One final statistic I wish to examine is the initial point of contact through which people come to participate in MSIA. In contrast to the stereotype of wandering "cult" members making new recruits from amongst the strangers they meet on street corners, most people become involved with a religious group — whether traditional or nontraditional — through family and friendship networks. Thus, I was not surprised to find the same pattern among MSIA members, over half of whom (55.4%) were introduced to the Movement by family or friends (Table 7.21). The second most often cited avenue by which people came into contact with MSIA was through Insight seminars (over a fourth: 28.4%).

Table 7.21 — Introduction to MSIA

1st Point of Contact	Count	Percent
Impersonal/Media	18	3.6
Friends/Relatives	227	55.4
Insight Seminar	142	28.4
Other	49	9.8
No Response	14	2.8
TOTAL	500	100.0

I was a little surprised to find that there was no statistically significant difference between current and former members on this questionnaire item. I had anticipated that proportionally more people who left the Movement would have initially been introduced to MSIA via some avenue other than friends or family. There was, however, less than a 1% difference between the two subsamples on this item (current members — 55.5% vs. former members — 54.7%). Thus, leaving MSIA has little or nothing to do with how one comes in.

Discussion

Given this demographic overview, as well as the Movement's beliefs and practices mentioned earlier in this chapter, the Movement of Spiritual Inner Awareness can be analyzed according to sociological "ideal types" of religious organizations, specifically the categories of cult, sect, and denomination. As in my earlier discussion, it should be borne in mind that I will be making use of the sociological meaning of the term "cult" as a form of social organization, rather than the popular, pejorative meaning of this term.

Ideologically, MSIA is consistent with the sociological definition of cult in that its themes tend to be mystical and esoteric. The centrality of John-Roger to the organization, his position as the primary source of the teachings, and his clear charismatic appeal are also cult-like characteristics (this despite the fact that J-R has consistently emphasized that the final authority for each person's life is himself/herself).

The Movement of Spiritual Inner Awareness distinguishes itself from sects and their call to reform a religious tradition (which is the defining trait of sects in classical sociological analysis); there is no message of reforming a particular religious tradition in MSIA, but rather an appeal to an eclectic and novel synthesis of elements from many traditions.

More important than its similarities, MSIA is at variance with the sociological definition of a cult in several significant ways. First and foremost, members are actively engaged in the world and concerned with the betterment of society. Second, MSIA does not deliberately contrast itself with dominant religious groups, but rather incorporates beliefs and practices from a number of religious traditions.

In its claim not to be totally novel, it distances itself from cults, which almost invariably claim a completely new teaching. (J-R has explicitly stated that MSIA is a "new look at ancient teachings.") Third, members are clearly not disenchanted with and alienated from the larger world, a common characteristic of both cults and sects. On the contrary, they tend to be well-educated, demonstrate stable employment, and value family relationships. Fourth, the organization itself appears to be beyond the cult stage of development in that MSIA is not remaining small and informal, does not appear to be transitory, and has already successfully navigated the passing of charismatic authority from J-R to John Morton. It remains to be seen how the organization will be affected by the founder's passing.

MSIA is highly consistent with the sociological profile of a denomination for the following reasons: First, it is tolerant of other denominations and recognizes the value of religious pluralism. MSIA has always been ecumenical and the organization is recognized as a cooperative "one among equals" by other religious movements. Second, members follow a fairly routinized daily "ritual" that does not encourage spontaneous emotional expression (e.g., as in a Pentecostal church) as part of one's spiritual practices. This has been true since its beginning. Third, the group trains a clergy. The existence of Peace Theological Seminary and College of Philosophy further reinforces MSIA's status as a denomination. Fourth, the organization accepts less extensive personal involvement from members than do either sects or cults. One can be a full member of the Movement of Spiritual Inner Awareness without participating in Church programs or in any other group activity.

Fifth, in its appeal to middle-aged individuals and its disproportionate draw from the middle class, the Church exhibits more of a prototypical image of a denomination than a cult. Sixth, MSIA tolerates internal theological debate. J-R has so often admonished students, "Don't believe what I say, check it out for yourself," that the phrase "check it out" is rampant among Movement members. Seventh, the pivotal characteristic which separates denominations from sects in classical sociological theory is that significant additions to membership come through birth to parents who are members. MSIA includes in its membership a large number of families, including children. As more and more children are included in the membership because of their parents' membership, the organization will move ever closer toward denominational status.

Lastly, the demography of the Movement of Spiritual Inner Awareness is more consistent with sociological definitions of denominations than of cults. Age patterns demonstrate a membership of several generations. Current marital status reflects a value for familism and an engagement in stable family life. (With respect to familism, I should also mention in passing that I have an impressionistic sense that MSIA participants tend to be meaningfully engaged with their non-MSIA parents.) Employment, occupation, and income levels describe a mature membership well integrated into the social and economic institutions of the larger society. Further, joining MSIA is not accompanied by any loss of occupational prestige or withdrawal from the larger society. Finally, multiple memberships in religious groups between childhood and membership in the Movement of Spiritual Inner Awareness indicate a serious lifelong search by most members for religious meaning and affiliation.

8

EX-MEMBERS AND THE "CULT" CONTROVERSY

*CULT LEADER JOHN-ROGER, WHO SAYS
HE'S INHABITED BY A DIVINE SPIRIT,
STANDS ACCUSED OF A CAMPAIGN OF HATE*

The above statement is the over-lengthy title of a lurid piece that was published in *People* magazine in the late eighties. Similar — though somewhat more cautious — articles have appeared in the *LA Times*, *Vanity Fair*, *The New Yorker*, *Playboy*, and others. Garry Trudeau even lampooned John-Roger in a series of "Doonesbury" cartoons in response to a congressional candidate whose wife had been linked to MSIA. As the stature of these periodicals indicates, the controversy surrounding J-R and his movement has attracted national attention. At least part of the media's attraction for MSIA's particular drama has been the manner in which the group has been drawn into the larger conflict surrounding minority religions — the so-called "cult" controversy.

We should note, however, that the media themselves contributed heavily to the emergence of this controversy as a public issue. Specifically, the journalistic penchant for sensationalism has played a decisive role in promoting the stereotype of "evil cults" to the larger society. The mass media is not, of course, motivated primarily by the quest for truth. Instead, the mainstream media is driven by market forces and by the necessity of competing with other newspapers, other TV news shows, and so forth.

This is not to say that reporters necessarily lie or fabricate their stories. Rather, in the case of minority religions, news people tend to accentuate beliefs, practices, or events that seem to be strange, dangerous, sensational, and the like because such portrayals titillate consumers of news. This kind of reporting contributes to the perpetuation of the cult stereotype. In the words of British sociologist James Beckford,

> *Journalists need no other reason for writing about any particular new religious movement except that it is counted as a cult. This categorization is sufficient to justify a story, especially if the story illustrates many of the other components which conventionally make up the "cult" category.*
>
> *This puts pressure on journalists to find more and more evidence which conforms with the categorical image of cults and therefore confirms the idea that a new religion is newsworthy to the extent that it does match the category. It is no part of conventional journalistic practice to look for stories about new religions which do not conform to the category of cult.*

Another important factor is the marked tendency of the mass media to report on a phenomenon only when it results in conflicts and problems. To again cite from Beckford,

> *New religious movements are only newsworthy when a problem occurs. Scandals, atrocities, spectacular failures, "tug-of-love" stories, defections, exposés, outrageous conduct — these are the main criteria of new religions' newsworthiness. . . . And, of course, the unspectacular, nonsensational new religions are permanently invisible in journalists' accounts.*

Once a dramatic story on a particular group appears in a major periodical, it becomes a point of reference for all subsequent stories on the same movement. This is because — given the deadlines for most stories, plus the budget constraints of most news media — few reporters have the time or the resources to collect original information. Instead, "research" consists of calling up information from previously published stories. And, because the data contained in earlier articles remain perpetually uncorrected, the same items of misinformation are repeated again and again, ad nauseam. Given enough time, the original misperceptions appear in so many publications that they acquire the weight of indisputable fact.

In the balance of the present chapter I will discuss the role of apostates (ex-members) in this controversy, focussing on the post-involvement attitudes of former participants in MSIA. The latter part of the chapter will examine the manner in which specific conflicts have been responsible for MSIA's assimilation into the "cult" stereotype.

Stepping off the Path

Since the mid-seventies, mainstream scholars — especially sociologists of religion — have been steadily churning out studies directly relevant to the cult controversy. (Because of the negative connotations of "cult," academics prefer to use the expression "new religious movement.") At this point in time, a collection of the books devoted to this controversy plus books on new religions containing at least one full chapter directly relevant to the controversy — and I mean a collection of mainstream scholarly works, not popular pseudo-studies — would form a stack 15 feet high. This does not include the large number of relevant articles published in academic journals. The anticult movement — by which I mean groups like the Cult Awareness Network (prior to its 1996 bankruptcy filing), the American Family Foundation, and so forth — has chosen to ignore this body of scholarly literature because it refutes the negative stereotypes they rely upon to justify their continued existence.

For example, the operative question that social scientists have asked with respect to the stereotype of cultic "mind control" is: How does one distinguish "cult brainwashing" from other forms of social influence — forms of social influence like advertising, military training, or even the normal socialization routines of the public schools? Some anticultists have theorized that members of minority religions are trapped in a kind of ongoing, quasi-hypnotic state, while others assert that the ability of members to process certain kinds of information has "snapped."

The problem with these and similar theories is that if cultic influences actually override the brain's ability to logically process information, then individuals suffering from cultic influences should perform poorly on I.Q. tests or, at the very least, should manifest pathological symptoms when they take standardized tests of mental health — but, when tested, they don't. In point of fact, such empirical studies indicate that members of new religious movements are actually smarter and healthier than the average member of mainstream American society.

Other kinds of studies also fail to support the anticultist view that new religions rely upon nonordinary forms of social influence to gain and retain members. For example, if new religions possessed powerful techniques of mind control that effectively override a potential convert's free will, then every one — or at least a large percentage — of the attendees at recruiting seminars should be unable to avoid conversion. However, sociologist Eileen Barker, in her important study, *The Making of a Moonie*, found that only a small percentage of the people attending seminars sponsored by the Unification Church — an organization many people regard as the "evil cult" par excellence — eventually joined. Furthermore, of those who joined, more than half dropped out within the first year of their membership. In another important study, Canadian psychiatrist Saul Levine found that, out of a sample of over 800 people who had joined controversial religious groups, more than 80% dropped out within two years of membership — not the kind of statistics one would anticipate in groups wielding powerful techniques of mind control.

In the face of these and other empirical studies, social scientists have asked the further questions of: Given the lack of empirical support, where does the brainwashing notion originate? And, what is the real nature of the conflict that the "cult" stereotype obscures? The general conclusion of sociologists (as analyzed in, for example, David Bromley and Anson Shupe's book-length study, *Strange Gods: The Great American Cult Scare*) is that the principal source of the controversy is a parent-child conflict in which parents fail to understand the choices of their adult children and attempt to reassert parental control by marshaling the forces of public opinion against the religious bodies to which their offspring have converted.

This core conflict is then exacerbated by an irresponsible mass media that is less interested in truth than in printing exciting stories about "weird cults" that trap their members and keep them in psychological bondage with exotic techniques of "mind control." Also, once an industry is established that generates substantial profits through the "rescue" of entrapped "cult" members (I am here referring, of course, to deprogramming), special-interest groups come into being that have a vested interest in promoting the most negative stereotypes of alternative religions. These special interest groups add further fuel to the parent-child conflict by scaring parents with lurid stories of what will happen to their adult child if they fail to have her or him deprogrammed. In this manner, many otherwise reasonable and well-meaning parents are recruited into the controversy.

Ex-members of nontraditional religious movements provide one of the keys to understanding the cult controversy. Groups opposed to religious minorities base much, if not all, of their attack on the testimony of former members who relate tales of manipulation and abuse. Former members who have "actually been there" and have supposedly witnessed all of the horrors about which outsiders can only fantasize, provide the cult stereotype with its most important source of empirical evidence. These narratives, anticultists would have us believe, give us insight into the real nature and purpose of cults, belying the benefic image minority religions project to the world.

In my research, I discovered that most voluntary defectors were ambivalent or even positive about their former religion, often characterizing their membership period as beneficial and enjoyable. In sharp contrast, people who had been involuntarily deprogrammed or in other ways counseled by anticultists described their membership and their former religion in terms of the popular negative stereotype of cults. The conclusion one must draw from these findings is that deprogramming is not the therapeutic intervention that it has been portrayed as, but, rather, an intensive indoctrination process in which the abductee's religious faith is systematically destroyed and replaced with anticult ideology. While I would never assert that there is nothing to be criticized in certain minority religions, a careful consideration of this conclusion should cause any thinking person to hesitate before accepting the more extreme accusations proffered by anticultists.

With respect to this controversy, one of the most striking aspects of MSIA is the manner in which it departs from the pattern of most other controversial minority religions. As I noted in an earlier chapter, membership in MSIA is not an all-or-nothing proposition, which sharply distinguishes the Movement from groups like the Moonies and the Hare Krishnas.

Largely as a consequence of MSIA's "low-demand" membership requirements (i.e., subscribing to Discourses is all that is needed to be considered an active member, and members are not required or even asked to change their lives in any way), members were rarely, if ever, viewed as brainwashed zombies by their parents and thus avoided being kidnapped off the streets and subjected to the inquisitional arts of deprogrammers. The pattern of the post-involvement attitudes of voluntary defectors, however, shed considerable light on MSIA and its relationship to the cult controversy. The Movement of Spiritual Inner Awareness's avoidance (until recently) of the cult controversy is reflected in former members' general lack of awareness of the anticult movement (ACM), an ignorance measured by two questionnaire items on the ex-member survey that requested (1) how one evaluated the ACM and (2) the extent of one's contact with the ACM. The first question asked was:

How would you evaluate "anticult" groups like the Cult Awareness Network?

1. Very Negative
2. More Negative than Positive
3. More Positive than Negative
4. Very Positive

More than anything else, the pattern of responses — such as they were — indicated a general lack of knowledge about anticult organizations (Table 8.1). Before examining the results, a couple of things should be pointed out about the results reported in the table.

First, a half-dozen people answered certain questionnaire items by simultaneously marking two adjacent responses (e.g., "1–2" instead of "1" or "2"), indicating that their attitude was somewhere between the two alternatives. Rather than deleting these respondents from the batch, my relatively small sample of completed Former Member Questionnaires (53) persuaded me to utilize such responses by assigning a half-point to each of the adjacent alternatives (an assignment that produced the ".5" values recorded in Table 8.1).

Second, note that percentage points have been rounded off to the nearest tenth of a percentage. As a consequence, the percentages in each table will not always add up to exactly 100%.

Finally, note that "N/R" means "Non-Response."

Table 8.1 — Attitude Toward Anticult Movement

	Count	Percent
1	8	15.1
2	17.5	33.0
3	2.5	4.7
4	3	5.7
N/R	22	41.5

The most striking aspect of responses to this item was the large number of people (more than two-fifths of the respondents) who chose to leave it blank. Eighteen of the twenty-two wrote something on the questionnaire beside the item like, "I have no information about it," "Don't know them," or "I'm not even aware of the Cult Awareness Network." In a couple of cases, respondents simply put a question mark in the blank provided for the answer.

My impression that most former MSIA members were largely uninformed about the cult controversy was reinforced by the item that measured the extent of one's contact with the ACM:

How would you describe the extent of your contact with "anticult" groups?

1. None
2. Minimal
3. Moderate
4. Extensive

Responses to this questionnaire item are tabulated in Table 8.2 below.

Table 8.2 — Contact with Anticult Movement

	Count	Percent
1	43	81.1
2	7	13.2
3	1	1.9
4	0	0.0
N/R	2	3.8

Over four-fifths (81.1%) of respondents had never been in direct contact with the anticult movement, and, of those who had, not a single respondent described her or his contact as "extensive." From answers to this item and to the first item, it is clear that few ex-members feel motivated to seek out the anticult movement after leaving MSIA.

We can isolate four key assertions that capture the essence of the negative stereotype through which minority religions are perceived: They recruit people by deceptive means; once recruited, they brainwash their members; their leadership is insincere; and their belief systems are bogus concoctions of the leader/founder. Four items on the former-member question-naire measured these attitudes. The first of these asked respon-dents how frequently they had described their socialization into MSIA as "brainwashing":

Do you ever use the term "brainwashed" to describe your involvement in MSIA?

1. Never
2. Rarely
3. Sometimes
4. Frequently or Always

Responses to this questionnaire item are tabulated in Table 8.3 below.

Table 8.3 — "Brainwashed"

	Count	Percent
1	43	81.1
2	4	7.5
3	4	7.5
4	1	1.9
N/R	1	1.9

This exaggerated pattern of response — over four-fifths of the sample asserting that they never described their MSIA indoctrination as "brainwashing" — is not surprising, given the general nonexposure of ex-members to anticult ideology. While almost everyone has come into contact with the cult stereotype via the mass media, the great majority of these respondents obviously did not feel that the stereotype fit their experience of MSIA. In other words, while many of these former members might believe that there are evil cults in society that attempt to snare innocent people and brainwash them, they clearly did not feel that they had been members of such a cult.

A closely related aspect of the negative stereotype of minority religions is that they deceptively recruit their members. The relevant item on the ex-member questionnaire requested respondents to describe the degree of deception/insincerity involved in their recruitment:

The people/events/literature that led you to become involved in MSIA was/were:

1. Mostly honest and sincere
2. Somewhat misleading
3. Very misleading
4. Completely deceptive and insincere

Responses to this questionnaire item are tabulated in Table 8.4 below.

Table 8.4 — Deceptive Recruitment

	Count	Percent
1	47	88.7
2	2	3.8
3	1	1.9
4	1	1.9
N/R	2	3.8

Like the brainwashing item, the pattern of response to this item presents us with a clear pattern, indicating that the great majority of these respondents do not feel that this aspect of the "evil cult" stereotype applies to their experience of MSIA any more than do sensationalistic notions of "cultic brainwashing."

What, then, one might ask, caused these ex-members to leave MSIA in the first place? Clearly their disaffiliation from MSIA rests on a significantly different basis than is expressed in the shallow categories of anticult ideology. We might well anticipate a less exaggerated pattern of responses on such items as a question asking respondents to evaluate the truth of MSIA's teachings. The relevant questionnaire item put the issue in terms of truth and falsity:

Which of the following best describes the teachings of MSIA?

1. Completely True
2. More True than False
3. More False than True
4. Completely False

Responses to this questionnaire item are tabulated in Table 8.5 below.

Table 8.5 — Evaluation of MSIA Teachings

	Count	Percent
1	8	15.1
2	38.5	72.6
3	3.5	6.6
4	2	3.8
N/R	1	1.9

Here we finally get something that begins to look like a statistical curve, even though more than 70% of the respondents marked the "More True than False" item. After carefully reading over the completed Former Member surveys, I came away feeling that I overstated responses One and Four. In other words, instead of wording the first and fourth choices "Completely True" and "Completely False," I should have worded them so as to read "Mostly or Completely True" and "Mostly or Completely False." Had I done so, I believe a number of the ex-members who marked response Two would have marked response One, resulting in a smoother distribution of responses.

Nevertheless, even given the response pattern recorded in Table 8.5, the attitudes of this sample of ex-members are much less rejecting of MSIA's teachings than one might anticipate. We might have reasonably expected more former members to dismiss the teachings as false. This expectation is, however, overly dependent on the model of the apostate who leaves a church because she or he has lost faith in religion altogether. By way of contrast, the typical ex-member of MSIA continues to adhere to those aspects of her or his belief system that are congruent with the larger metaphysical/occult/New Age sub-culture — and the area of overlap between the teachings and the general ideology of the metaphysical subculture is fairly extensive. Thus, in the great majority of cases, leaving MSIA is more like dropping out of a Baptist Church and then joining a Pentecostal Church than it is like leaving religion entirely. This explains why most ex-members would describe the teachings as "More True than False."

What, then, about former members' attitudes toward John-Roger, the founder of MSIA, whose unique spiritual role is one of the principal points on which MSIA's teachings depart from generic metaphysical ideology? Might ex-members hold more negative attitudes toward J-R than toward MSIA teachings more generally? The relevant questionnaire item puts the issue in the following terms:

Which of the following best describes John-Roger Hinkins?

1. A Great Spiritual Leader
2. A Generally O.K. Spiritual Leader
3. A Substandard Spiritual Leader with a few good points
4. Completely Deluded or Completely False

Responses to this questionnaire item are tabulated in Table 8.6 below.

Table 8.6 — Evaluation of John-Roger

	Count	Percent
1	11	20.8
2	24.5	46.3
3	10.5	19.8
4	2	3.8
N/R	5	9.4

Here we finally get a pattern of responses that looks something like a normal statistical curve. Nevertheless, over two-thirds of the sample were still willing to give John-Roger a "Great" to "O.K." rating, despite the fact that they left the Movement. Only two former members were willing to describe J-R as "false" or "deluded," and at least one of these ex-members converted to conservative Christianity after leaving MSIA.

This surprising statistic indicates that, although all 53 respondents had left MSIA, most felt they benefited in one way or another from their participation in the Movement. Because they value the time they spent in the Movement, the majority feel no particular need to engage in self-justifying criticisms of either the teachings or John-Roger. This feeling of having benefited from involvement was explicitly measured by an open-ended item on the questionnaire that asked respondents if their MSIA involvement had helped or hurt them:

How has your involvement in MSIA influenced your life, for better or for worse?

Responses to this questionnaire item are tabulated in Table 8.7 below.

Table 8.7 — Better/Worse for the Experience

	Count	Percent
Better	38	71.1
Worse	4	7.8
Mixed	3	5.7
Neither	6	11.3
N/R	2	3.8

With almost three-fourths of the sample willing to assert unambiguously that they feel they are better off for having been participants in MSIA, it is easy to see how so few ex-members feel a need to castigate the Movement, the teachings, or the founder. This situation is perfectly understandable if, as I have already indicated, we realize that most of the people who have left MSIA still consider themselves "on the path," in the larger sense, and continue to participate in some form of metaphysical/New Age spirituality. Such people can thus regard their membership period as part of their larger quest, and, as a consequence, positively value the time and energy they invested in MSIA. The pattern of responses to one final questionnaire item that assessed the value of the membership period further reinforces this interpretation. This item asked respondents to imaginatively place themselves back in time at the point where they initially became involved in MSIA:

If you could be transported back to the time you began your involvement with MSIA, you would probably

1. Do it all over again with few or no changes
2. Do it all over again with many changes
3. Not get so deeply involved
4. Not get involved at all

Responses to this questionnaire item are tabulated in Table 8.8 below.

Table 8.8 — Would You Do It All Over Again?

	Count	Percent
1	32	60.4
2	5	9.4
3	5	9.4
4	7	13.2
N/R	4	7.5

Here once again we have an exaggerated pattern of response. In this particular case, the majority of the sample (about three-fifths) asserted that, if they had their membership period to do over again, they would "do it all over again with few or no changes."

Social Functions of the Cult Stereotype

In studying the conflict between new religious movements (NRM) and their most persistent critic — the so-called anticult movement (ACM) — sociologically informed observers have tended to focus on the efforts of the ACM to gain widespread social acceptance for its peculiar perspective on nontraditional religious groups. Because the consensus among mainstream NRM scholars is that the most dramatic claims made by the ACM against minority religions are inaccurate, many analysts have adopted a critical stance, attempting to uncover the deeper interests lying behind ACM rhetoric about brainwashing, cultic manipulation, and the like. These discussions of the ACM, and of the cult stereotype propagated by the ACM, have drawn on recent theorizing about social movements — theorizing that has tended to focus on the "macro" (in the sense of general, overall) dynamics of such movements. This tendency to emphasize what takes place at the broader levels of society has been prompted by, among other factors, a reaction among social scientists against earlier "micro" (in the sense of individualistic) theorizing that gave excessive attention to explaining why individuals become involved in social movements.

In my own research, I have become interested in understanding how particular minority religions are drawn into the "cult wars," as well as how ACM ideology is used in specific conflicts involving individuals and groups who, for the most part, have no interest in the wider ACM crusade. To understand social dynamics at this level, which lies somewhere between the "macro" level of the larger ACM and the "micro" level of individual involvement, some adaptation of earlier theorizing is called for. In the balance of the present chapter I will undertake to examine some of the specific conflicts through which the Church of the Movement of Spiritual Inner Awareness has been drawn into the cult controversy. For most of the people involved in conflicts with MSIA, the cult stereotype is an ideological resource, useful for eliciting support for their side of the struggle, but representing no deep involvement in the anticult cause.

The anticult movement's most powerful sphere of influence is in the arena of helping to construct and reinforce negative stereotypes about nontraditional religions in the mass media. However, the popularity of the cult stereotype indicates that there is a preexisting disposition to accept such stereotypes in American society. By attending to certain themes in anticult discourse, it should be possible to uncover some of the factors behind the receptivity of contemporary society to negative, stereotyped images of minority religions. Relevant social-psychological research also indicates that once a stereotype has been accepted, it structures our perceptions so that we tend to notice information that conforms to our image of the stereotyped group and to neglect or forget other kinds of information. What this means for any given confrontation is that as soon as the label "cult" has been successfully applied (i.e., accepted as appropriate by outsiders not directly involved in the conflict), the information that the mass media gathers is selectively appropriated so that almost every item of data conforms to the stereotype about cults, thus effectively marshaling moral support for the person or group locked in conflict with a minority religion. Finally, in the last section of this chapter, I will deal directly with the accusations leveled against John-Roger and MSIA that cannot simply be dismissed as a function of the cult stereotype.

What is a stereotype? Stereotypes are generalizations about other groups of people, but they are a peculiar type of generalization, characterizing whole groups of people inaccurately. Stereotypes are also usually held rigidly, in that we tend to ignore or to dismiss evidence that flies in the face of our generalization. Such rigidity indicates that our stereotypes may be protecting our self-esteem or helping us to avoid facing up to some unpleasant fact. Thus the stereotype of certain races as "lazy," for example, would simultaneously boost the self-esteem of society's dominant racial group as well as blind one to the inequalities of existing social arrangements. It is relatively easy to perceive that most generalizations about cults are little more than negative stereotypes, but what are the social forces that make such stereotypes about nontraditional religions peculiarly attractive to contemporary society?

Unless there are groups that are consciously antisocial or criminal like the Mafia or like gangs, the deviations from the norm that a community chooses to perceive as threatening are somewhat arbitrary. The people that our culture has traditionally construed as deviants have been racial (e.g., Blacks), ethnic (e.g., Jews), and sexual (e.g., homosexuals) minorities. In recent years, however, it has become socially unacceptable to persecute these traditional groups, at least in the overt manner in which they have been attacked in the past. This leaves few groups of any significant size to persecute. One of the few minorities that liberals (traditional defenders of the underdog) have been slow to defend are nontraditional religions. This is due to a number of different factors, including the resistance of traditionally conservative religions to liberal change. The failure of normally open-minded people to protect religious pluralism has allowed contemporary witch hunters to declare open season on cults.

Groups of people that are regarded as threatening frequently become screens onto which a society projects its anxieties. If, for example, a culture is troubled by sexual issues (as is often the case), then its enemies are perceived as perverse, sexually deviant, and so forth. Racial minorities, who have often been viewed as "loose" and sexually aggressive, have suffered from this projection. This was also a dominant theme in nineteenth century anti-Catholic and anti-Mormon literature. Contemporary cults, of course, suffer from the same projection.

In his classical formulation of the notion of psychological projection, Freud, who was especially concerned with sex and violence, viewed projection as a defense mechanism against unacceptable inner urges. Thus, in a society with strict sexual mores, an individual constantly keeping a lid on his desires might perceive rather ordinary dancing, let us say, as sexually suggestive. Becoming enraged at such "loose" behavior, he might then attempt to lead a movement to have all of the dance halls in town closed down. It should be clear that this hypothetical individual's inner struggle is being "projected" outward to provide a script for an outer struggle (i.e., internally he is repressing his desires while symbolically battling the same desires in the outer world). The same process is at work in the collective mind of society, perceiving marginal groups as sexually deviant. For instance, the stereotype of the sexually abusive cult leader, routinely forcing devotees to satisfy his or her sexual whims, perfectly captures the fantasy of those members of our society who desire to sexually control any person he or she wishes.

The same kind of process occurs with respect to repressed aggressive urges. We live in a society with strict sanctions against overt violence; simultaneously, violence is glorified in the entertainment media. This sets up a cultural contradiction that can then be projected onto enemies and deviant groups, with the result that minorities are often perceived as violent and belligerent. This accusation is also regularly projected onto nontraditional religions. In particular, the violent actions of a tiny handful of members of alternative religions is mistakenly taken to indicate a widespread tendency among all such groups.

We can generalize beyond Freudian psychology's emphasis on sex and aggression to see that many other cultural anxieties/cultural contradictions are projected onto minority groups. For instance, our society gives us contradictory messages about the relative importance of wealth and material success. On the one hand, we are taught that economic pursuits

208 *James R. Lewis*

should be secondary to higher moral, social, and spiritual concerns. On the other hand, we receive many messages from the surrounding society that the single-minded pursuit of wealth is the be-all and end-all of life. This inherent contradiction is typically ignored or overlooked with regard to mainstream religions where gross economic inequities exist within the same community or where religious elites enjoy favored status and privilege. Instead of being faced directly, this self-contradiction is examined only after it has been projected onto alternative religions, where it constitutes the basis of the stereotype of the money-hungry cult leader who demands that his or her followers lead lives of poverty while the leader wallows in riches.

One of the more important cultural contradictions projected onto alternative religions is reflected in the brainwashing/mind-control notion that is the core accusation leveled against such groups. Discourse that glorifies American society usually does so in terms of a rhetoric of liberty and freedom. However, while holding liberty as an ideal, we experience a social environment that is often quite restrictive. Most citizens work as employees in highly disciplined jobs where the only real freedom is the freedom to quit. Also, we are daily bombarded by advertising designed to influence our decisions and even to create new needs. Our frustration with these forms of influence and control is easily displaced and projected onto the separated societies of alternative religions.

The components of the cult stereotype that have been enumerated above, and others that could be mentioned, explain certain themes in anticult discourse, as well as why this stereotype tends to resonate with public opinion. Without this pre-existing disposition to construe nontraditional religions negatively, the anticult movement would have little or no social influence. However, even this influence is limited, in the sense that the stereotype the ACM has helped to shape has taken on a life of its own, independent of organized anticultism.

In their role as "moral entrepreneurs," ACM spokespersons have effectively marketed their negative stereotype of minority religions to the general public. Because of the preexisting fit between this negative image and the persistent social anxieties outlined in this section, our society has overwhelmingly bought into the stereotype (or purchased the moral commodity, to continue the entrepreneurial metaphor). Because of widespread acceptance of the stereotype, the ACM could disappear tomorrow and anticult discourse would still continue to shape public perceptions of minority religions.

Once a stereotype is in place, a variety of different kinds of studies have shown that it becomes self-fulfilling and self-reinforcing. Thus, in a study by Snyder and Uranowitz, for example, students were asked to read a short biography about Betty K., a fictitious woman. Her life story was constructed so that it would fulfill certain stereotypes of both heterosexuals and lesbians. In Snyder's words, "Betty, we wrote, never had a steady boyfriend in high school, but did go out on dates. And although we gave her a steady boyfriend in college, we specified that he was more of a close friend than anything else." A week later, they told some of the students that Betty was currently living with her husband, and another group of students that she was living with another woman in a lesbian relationship. When subsequently requested to answer a series of questions about Betty, they found a marked tendency on the part of students to reconstruct her biography so as to conform to stereotypes about either heterosexuality or homosexuality, depending on the information they had received.

Those who believed that Betty was a lesbian remembered that Betty had never had a steady boyfriend in high school, but tended to neglect the fact that she had gone out on many dates in college. Those who believed that Betty was now a heterosexual, tended to remember that she had formed a steady relationship with a man in college, but tended to ignore the fact that this relationship was more of a friendship than a romance.

More directly relevant to the case at hand is an important article by Jeffrey E. Pfeifer reporting the results of a similar study that compared responses to a biography in which a fictitious student, Bill, dropped out of college to enter a Catholic seminary, join the Marines, or join the Moonies. The short biography incorporated elements of indoctrination often attributed to cults, such as:

> *While at the facility, Bill is not allowed very much contact with his friends or family and he notices that he is seldom left alone. He also notices that he never seems to be able to talk to the other four people who signed up for the program and that he is continually surrounded by [Moonies, Marines, Priests] who make him feel guilty if he questions any of their actions or beliefs.*

When given a choice of describing Bill's indoctrination experience, subjects who thought Bill had joined the Catholic priesthood most often labeled his indoctrination "resocialization"; those who were told that he had joined the Marines most frequently labeled the process "conversion"; and those who were under the impression that he had become a Moonie applied the label "brainwashing." On various other questions regarding the desirability and fairness of the indoctrination process, subjects who were told that Bill had joined the Moonies consistently evaluated his experience more negatively than subjects who were under the impression that Bill had joined either the Marines or a priestly order. The implication of this analysis is that minority religions lose their chance for a fair hearing as soon as the label cult is successfully applied to them. After that, the news media selectively seeks out and presents information that fits the stereotype. It is then only a matter of time before the group in question is completely "demonized."

While the cult stereotype has come to dominate public discourse about minority religions, and while groups like the Unification Church and People's Temple seem to have become integral parts of that stereotype, there is enough ambiguity in the cult label to make its application in particular cases a matter of negotiation. Occasions for such negotiation arise in the context of social conflicts. For individuals or groups locked in certain kinds of struggles with members of minority religions, the cult stereotype represents a potent ideological resource which — if they are successful in making the label stick — marshals public opinion against their opponent, potentially tipping the balance of power in their favor.

Situations in which this strategy can work are not restricted to the kinds of conflicts that are picked up by the news media. For example, the stigma of the cult stereotype has been effectively deployed in child custody cases, in which one parent's membership in a minority religion is portrayed as indicative of her or his unworthiness as a parent. For such "limited domain" legal conflicts, however, it is difficult to deploy the stereotype unless there is some larger, earlier conflict that led to press coverage in which the particular minority religion in question was labeled a cult. Lacking earlier "bad press," the cult label can still sometimes be made to stick on the basis of testimony by disgruntled former members.

For the most part, individuals involved in such relatively limited conflicts do not become full-time ACM crusaders. While they may enter into a relationship with the ACM, they normally drift away from this involvement within a short time after the termination of their particular struggle. To refer back to the entrepreneurial model, these people are not so much moral entrepreneurs as they are consumers of a moral commodity — they have "purchased" a prepackaged cult stereotype and brought it to bear as one tool in their array of resources. They may, of course, still have to exercise persuasive skills in getting the public or the court to accept the applicability of the stereotype, but otherwise they are not invested in the product per se. If anticult rhetoric fails to accomplish their end, but some other tool works in their particular conflict, they are usually quite ready to dispose of the cult stereotype and adopt an entirely different angle of attack.

For example, in the mountains overlooking Santa Barbara, California, the Foundation for the Study of Individual and World Peace (or IIWP, an organization founded by John-Roger) purchased some property — later named Windermere — for the purpose of building a peace retreat facility. Bordered on one side by a national forest, their property is also directly adjacent to a semirural neighborhood populated by individuals who moved away from the city for the purpose of enjoying country living. Some of these people view their new neighbor with concern. When they heard about plans to build a facility that, they imagined, would attract large numbers of outsiders from the Los Angeles area who would disturb their peaceful rural setting, some were upset. Eventually some neighbors organized the Cielo Preservation Organization (named after the main road in the area) to oppose the construction of the retreat — construction that cannot proceed without approval from the county.

Not long after a negative article about MSIA appeared in the *Los Angeles Times*, almost everyone in the neighborhood received a copy. This slanted article immediately became a centerpiece in some of the neighbors' opposition to IIWP's retreat plans. By 1994, the *Times*' report had been superseded by the considerable publicity Arianna Huffington's MSIA connections were generating in the southern California media. Thus, in a December 1994 article in the local Santa Barbara paper on the conflict between Windermere and the neighborhood, Huffington and her cult connections were brought up and discussed near the beginning of the article:

>His [John-Roger's] teachings drew national attention
>during this year's California Senate race between
>incumbent Diane Feinstein and Rep. Michael
>Huffington because the Montecito congressman's
>wife, Arianna, had ties to the John-Roger organiza-
>tion, which some critics claim is a cult. Arianna
>Huffington has said it is not a cult, and described her
>past connection with MSIA as a casual one.

Despite the cautious wording of this passage, the net effect
of mentioning such accusations is that otherwise uninformed
readers may conclude that the "cult" label is probably appropriate for MSIA, thus influencing them to side with the
retreat's opponents.

I happen to live just down the mountain from Windermere,
and, to judge from my conversations with local residents, this
labeling enterprise has been highly successful in generating
anti-IIWP/anti-MSIA sentiment in Santa Barbara county. The
point here, however, is that the Cielo Preservation
Organization is less concerned about the ranch owners' religious persuasion than about preventing, in the words of a local
organizer, hordes of "L.A. cowboys" from invading the area,
thus spoiling their rural privacy. The claim that the
Windermere Ranch is populated by "weird cultists" is what I
have termed an ideological resource or a moral commodity —
simply one among many accusations hurled at IIWP in an all-
out effort to short circuit their retreat plans.

The mention of the Huffingtons in the Santa Barbara paper
alludes to an entirely different type of struggle that provides
yet another example of the marshaling of the cult stereotype
for deployment in a conflict not directly involving the ACM.
The Feinstein-Huffington campaign for the U.S. Senate was a
particularly bitter fight, with both camps relying heavily on

expensive, negative TV ads. For a number of reasons, however, the media seemed to take more offense at Michael Huffington's bid for Senator than at Diane Feinstein's efforts to defend her seat in Congress. For one thing, and this may have been his biggest "sin" in the eyes of reporters, he consistently refused to be interviewed by what he felt to be a biased liberal media. Instead, Huffington attempted to bypass the news media altogether, appealing directly to voters through television advertisements. Rebuffed by the Huffington camp, the news media responded by characterizing Michael Huffington as a wealthy outsider attempting to buy a Senate seat, and, more generally, sought out and reported whatever negative bits of information they could find on this Republican challenger.

When Arianna Huffington's connection with MSIA was discovered, the mass media in southern California immediately jumped on the information. Uncritically repeating accusations from the 1988 *Los Angeles Times* piece, reporters quickly transformed Michael Huffington's senatorial bid from an outsider trying to buy his way into the U.S. Senate, into the machinations of an evil cult leader working behind the scenes through the candidate's wife to gain political influence for himself and his cult agenda. This absurd accusation was repeated (though sometimes subtly and by implication) in a number of articles, including important pieces in *The New Yorker* and *Vanity Fair*. Few reporters bothered to look more deeply into John-Roger and MSIA, much less question the appropriateness of the cult stereotype. Neither did they tend to emphasize that Mr. Huffington never had anything to do with MSIA.

Instead, as one might have anticipated, reporters' preexisting disposition to perceive Huffington negatively led them to accept accusations of his "cult connection" without further reflection. It was then almost inevitable that, as prior research into the self-fulfilling nature of stereotypes would have predicted, any new information gathered on MSIA would be filtered through the cult image.

However, while the news media is not particularly interested in uncovering the truth about minority religions, neither is it particularly interested in joining with the ACM to undertake a protracted campaign to destroy minority religions. Ultimately, the mass media is primarily concerned about making a profit and, to the extent that the cult image helps them to accomplish this end, the media buys into — and, in turn, propagates — the stereotype as a moral commodity.

To conclude this overview of MSIA-related conflicts with one final example, I have already mentioned that the "cult" stereotype has been effectively deployed in some child custody cases. In the words of Michael Homer, an expert in legal cases involving minority religions:

> *Religious practices and beliefs have also become the subject of child custody cases where nonmembers attempt to highlight nontraditional aspects of a spouse's or ex-spouse's religion to obtain custody of a minor child. Nonmembers seek to show that the religion deviates from social normalcy and, therefore, adversely affects the child's behavior. It is argued that the church's influence is mentally, physically, and emotionally detrimental to the child's well-being. Nonmembers have been successful when the court determines that the practices complained of are not merely religious but are detrimental practices that harm the child.*

In one case of which I am aware, a parent's association with MSIA was effectively used against her by the other parent in a dispute involving their mutual offspring. In this particular case, a divorced mother petitioned the court to permit her to relocate in order to take a position in an MSIA-inspired organization offering human potentials seminars. The ex-husband argued that he did not want his son involved in a cult, and dragged up all of the old rumors about John-Roger and MSIA in an effort to prevent his ex-wife from leaving the state. Perceiving that not only would she have a difficult time winning her case, but also that her husband might undertake further actions that could result in her son being taken from her, she dropped the case.

What is especially ironic about this case is that for several decades the father has been deeply involved in est — a human potentials group that has very frequently (far more frequently than MSIA) been labeled a cult. As someone whose participation in est has likely sensitized him to the cult controversy, the ex-husband's utilization of the stereotype is clearly little more than a tactic intended to win support for his side of the case, rather than a reflection of deeply held views about the dangers of sinister cults. As the mother said to me in a telephone interview, she feels that her former spouse was advised to "shoot her where you think you can hurt her," and that her involvement in a MSIA-related organization was simply a convenient target.

The chances of this gentleman becoming a full-time ACM crusader are practically nil. Here, as in the other instances we have examined, it is clear that the cult stereotype is an ideological resource, used without a deep investment in the stereotype per se. This way of understanding the cult image's role in particular struggles represents a variation on earlier theorizing. As I have already indicated, most recent theorizing has focused on the ACM's campaign to win acceptance of both its ideology and its agenda by the greater society. By shifting the point of focus from this broad level to more particular struggles, we were able to see that, in the context of grass roots conflicts, the cult stereotype becomes a moral commodity — an ideological resource that can easily be set aside if it is not persuasive, or if some other tactic better suits the situation.

As earlier sections of this book have demonstrated, participants appropriate the teachings and practices of MSIA, integrate them into their lives, and experience authentic self-transformation. With the exception of certain secularists who feel that all forms of religion are bad, and the exception of exclusivistic religionists who believe that only one religion leads to salvation, I think any reasonable observer would have to conclude that MSIA fulfills all of the criteria for a genuine religious movement.

Some people will, however, continue to ask questions along the lines of, What if John-Roger just "made up" the teachings? And, What if John-Roger really did sexually exploit some of his personal staff members? Questions like these cannot, in the final analysis, be answered to everyone's satisfaction. So, rather than defending or accusing John-Roger, let me turn these questions around and instead ask: If these accusations were true, what difference would it make? In other words, if we knew for certain that John-Roger just invented MSIA's teachings and committed acts like sexually exploiting some of his followers, would that indicate — as some critics imply — that the whole religion was therefore inauthentic and should be abandoned?

If we examine the historical record, we find that the question of a religion's authenticity has rarely been decided on the basis of the good or bad intentions/actions of a religious group's founder. I was, for example, raised in the Episcopal Church, which originated as a schism from the Anglican Church. The Anglican Church, in turn, was originally founded by the king of England primarily because the Pope had refused to allow him to divorce his wife. Few people would be prepared to denounce Episcopalianism as bad or inauthentic because of the less-than-noble motives of its founder. This is at least partially because the Anglican Church continued a pre-existing religious tradition with few changes.

Most new religions, in fact, begin as variations on preexisting religions. As a consequence, such religions draw on time-tested ideas, practices, and values. Thus, even so-called false prophets tend to preach messages containing more light than darkness. In the case at hand, it is clear that John-Roger has drawn heavily from the universal storehouse of religious inspiration. Whatever his intentions, his teachings resonate with universal truth. In my ongoing contact with Movement participants, I have, furthermore, experienced noble individuals following a noble teaching that has transformed many people's lives for the better. If the test of the authenticity of a religion deals with how people live their lives, then I would classify MSIA as an authentic religion. And I would stand by this judgment even if I became convinced that John-Roger had made up MSIA from whole cloth.

As for the allegation of sexual exploitation, there has been revelation after revelation in recent years about Catholic clergymen using their position of authority to sexually exploit boys and young men. In spite of this documented abuse, no one stands up and seriously proposes, on the basis of such incidents, that Catholicism is not an authentic religion which should therefore be abandoned. Nor is anyone prepared to assert that all of the marriages, baptisms, and so forth performed by errant priests are invalid because of the clergymen's deviant activities (and must henceforth be redone). Why should the criterion be any different for leaders of small, non-traditional religious movements? Whatever personal "sins" John-Roger might have committed — and none have been proven — they would not, in themselves, invalidate MSIA.

To shift away from John-Roger to his organization, I must say that, when compared with other movements stigmatized as destructive cults, MSIA is one of the most innocuous groups I have ever studied. MSIA does not, for example, ask members to quit their schooling or to quit their job. Members do not abandon their families, nor do they spend their spare time fundraising and recruiting new members. Their diet does not change upon joining, they do not have to cut their hair in a certain way, and they do not have to wear distinctive clothing in order to participate fully in MSIA. On the contrary, MSIA specifically states that all of these things and anything else relating to a person's physical life (what J-R has called the "10% level") is up to each person to decide for himself/herself. In fact, as with joining any mainstream denomination, almost nothing changes in one's lifestyle when one becomes involved in this church.

Given the lack of outward requirements, I have a difficult time imagining how the organization would go about operationalizing "destructiveness" even if the group's leadership decided it wanted MSIA to start acting like a destructive cult — it would be like the Elks Club trying to transform itself into a destructive cult. There are, in other words, few arenas within which one could exercise abusive power unless one completely reorganized the group.

9

EPILOG: A LOOK TO THE FUTURE

How, then, do we live in this world?
How can we gain?
What can our goal be?

For God's sake,
*   don't have a goal in this world.*
It's going to beat you bloody.

Where is the goal?
The goal is inside.
When you turn back inside,
*   you have your goal,*
*   you have your completeness,*
*   you have your fullness*
*   and you walk through the world,*
*   having all else added unto you.*
                                    —John-Roger

One of the perennial issues among scholars who study emergent religious movements is the question of a given movement's long-term viability, particularly its perceived ability to weather the passing of the founder. Another, related question is a movement's perceived growth-potential, which is viewed as a sign of its vitality.

MSIA has already experienced a smooth transition of spiritual authority from John-Roger to John Morton. Some members were surprised that Morton was picked to receive the mantle of the Mystical Traveler, but no one fundamentally questioned the transition. Also, as a corporate church structure, MSIA functions independently of John-Roger and John Morton, indicating that the process sociologists refer to as the "routinization of charisma" (the passing of charismatic authority from the founder to the organization) is already well underway. If J-R were to pass on tomorrow, I am confident that the day-to-day functioning of MSIA as an organization would continue with few ripples. This is especially likely because John Morton has already taken on some of the spiritual leadership of the group.

As for growth, in the 1970s MSIA expanded rapidly until it had grown to about five thousand members. At that point growth in total numbers stopped. Over the years people have come and gone, while overall membership figures have remained about the same. In terms of this nonexpansion, MSIA presents a profile of being like a traditional community in the Hindu tradition centered around a guru and his intimate disciples. Normally, this kind of a movement does not attempt to grow beyond a close community of teacher and students. As one MSIA participant told me,

> *People can come to seminars, but there are certain people that are here specifically because they've done*

a number of lifetimes in which they have acquired a particular kind of training. They're here for a very specific kind of ministry. I don't think MSIA is supposed to be big in numbers. I think it's just what it is, and, to me, [size is not a criterion of] success or failure.

This individual further portrayed MSIA as one among many "mystery schools," and only a certain number of people on the earth belonged to this particular school. Using this model as a lens through which to view MSIA, it is not surprising that the group has essentially the same number of members as it did twenty years ago. From another point of view, it is clear that MSIA has the capacity to become much larger. The Sikh religion, for example, began as a traditional guru-based community and later expanded to become a world religion.

Over the course of this study, I asked many different people how they viewed the future of MSIA. After collecting a wide range of different responses, the overall impression was what I can only describe as a Movement-wide ambivalence about growth. This ambivalence about growth reflects MSIA's ambivalence about action in the world more generally. In other words, as the organization's name indicates, MSIA is concerned primarily with the development of the kind of inner awareness that leads to Soul Transcendence. For the sake of reaching this ultimate goal, students are taught to remain detached from more worldly goals and purposes, a teaching reflected in the passage cited above.

Simultaneously, students are encouraged to be active in the world, and to contribute to the goal of transforming the world into a better place. John-Roger has stated many times that, "Service is the highest form of consciousness on the planet." MSIA participants consistently develop ministerial service projects that include feeding the homeless, tutoring, teaching, visiting the elderly, the sick, the imprisoned, and the lonely. In addition to these practical, physical ministries in their communities, MSIA participants are encouraged to pray for and to visualize improved conditions in their families, neighborhoods, countries, and the world, for the highest good of all.

One of the very first pieces I read in the *New Day Herald*, MSIA's in-house newspaper, was an article about how Light Bearers (meaning MSIA members as well as people following other, similar paths) were contributing to the upliftment of the world — a spiritual activity reflected in such external events as the fall of the Berlin Wall. To cite a passage from this article:

> *A trip to Russia in 1988 was followed closely by that country's leader moving toward openness in all parts of his domain: USSR, Baltic countries, Czechoslovakia, Hungary and even Rumania! J-R spent some time in Poland, met Lech Walesa, and Walesa emerged as an eloquent and humorous spokesperson for change. We connected with Archbishop Desmond Tutu, J-R visited South Africa, and dramatic positive change has been taking place there between the races.*
>
> *Then there's the Berlin Wall. The videotapes came back from the 1988 trip with participants singing, "J-R put a worm in the Berlin Wall, the Berlin Wall, the Berlin Wall, J-R put a worm in the Berlin Wall, and the wall came tumbling down!"*

The worm in this passage refers to the "Light Worm" of positive, spiritual energy that John-Roger asked MSIA people to visualize eating away at the Berlin Wall.

Clearly the author of this piece believes it was the activity of J-R and MSIA that tipped the scales on everything from remarkable changes in South Africa to the fall of the Iron Curtain. This belief, which most readers of the *New Day Herald* presumably share, reflects both a faith in the efficacy of the activity of Light Bearers and a belief that Light Bearers should, in fact, be working for a better world. While John-Roger himself rarely addresses such matters, he has occasionally portrayed MSIA — or, at least, members of MSIA — as playing a key role in the history of the unfoldment of the planet; for example, from *The Christ Within*:

> *It is our destinies this time on the planet to lift the consciousness of the world and actually prepare it for the golden age that is now approaching. Those of us in MSIA are that golden bridge from the consciousness of yesterday to the consciousness of tomorrow.*

Though this belief does not contradict the directive to focus one's energy on achieving Soul Transcendence, clearly there is potential for tension between MSIA's other-worldly goals and its this-worldly ideals. For instance, as I asserted earlier, I sense that the organization's ambivalence about growth is ultimately rooted in the teachings' ambivalence about action in the world.

Toward the end of this study, I had a long interview with John-Roger and John Morton. By that point, I already had answers to many of my earlier queries. There were, however, still unanswered questions regarding the future of MSIA. As a consequence, much of the interview was taken up with questions about this future, including questions about MSIA's potential for future expansion. What follows are some of the relevant excerpts — edited for readability — from this interview:

Lewis: As I look back over the couple of decades of MSIA's existence, what I see is that in some ways it's like a traditional Indian movement centered around a guru — one that does not attempt to grow beyond a small community of teacher and students. But in other ways I look at MSIA and feel it has the capacity of becoming much larger. Sikhism, for example, is said to have begun as a Sant Mat group, and it eventually became a world religion.

So as I've looked at MSIA, I've asked people like Paul Kaye and Mark Lurie [members of the Church presidency], "Do you see yourself remaining around the size of five or six thousand people, or do you see yourself really expanding and becoming more and more a force on the planet, having more members and growing into a different kind of organization?" Let me set the stage for this question a little bit more.

Some of the older students who have been with MSIA for a long time don't like the fact that it's not as informal as it used to be. The organization has gone from something like a small group of people hanging out around J-R to more and more of a formal organization. Some of these older students dislike the fact that some of the earlier physical intimacy has been lost. But at the same time, now that it's less centered on J-R's personal presence, it has more of an expansive possibility. So, what is your vision, or visions, of the future?

John Morton: I don't have a clear vision that's so identifiable. I have a sense of what I'm looking at, from here forward. In other words, the question to me would be, "What's up ahead for MSIA?" And maybe I'll only be able to get to next week. And you'd say, "Well, I was really interested in something like five, ten, twenty-five years from now." And maybe I'll be able to see something beyond that.

I don't have a direct answer other than the way I look at what happens to people is that they are Spirit-directed. The people who stay with us and endure are people who have a spiritual contact. They get a real inner experience that holds them and sustains them. It's absolutely what happens to each individual if they're really going to partake in the Movement of Spiritual Inner Awareness. So I have to defer the answer to the Spirit. That is what I look to, what we answer to.

Someone could say, "Well, that's easy for you to say, because anybody can put on a hat, a turban, or a robe and declare whatever, and some people will believe it and some people won't believe it." You can get people to do all kinds of things based on what you say. People will respond to forms of rhetoric and do all kinds of things. I think there's plenty of history to support that point.

But I don't look at what we teach as an artificial hodge-podge, which is what John-Roger's been accused of doing. Church critics charge that he has taken things from Sant Mat or Eckankar or Christianity — that he grew up as a Mormon and then he dabbled in this and then he dabbled in that, and he read this and he read that, and he just kind of concocted it. They say, "You don't really have any substance, you just have something that's a shell." But that's not been my experience.

What you're asking is, "Is this a growing movement in which more people are going to participate?" And I think, of course, why not? Because there's a fountain here, there's something that's rich and nourishing of the Spirit, and it's available to people, so why wouldn't they?

Presently I think that there are a lot of distractions that keep the Movement at a status-quo level. In the last ten years the number of people on Discourses has been relatively constant. If you look at it in terms of geography, it shifts around. But the actual base of people on Discourses, studying towards initiation and that type of thing, is relatively the same. Has the information shifted significantly? No. You can see some shift over the years, but the essential message, the essential direction, is the same.

We have a mission statement for the Church, which is, in part, "making the teachings available to those who are looking for them." The most important segment of that are the people already involved in MSIA. They're still looking for the teachings, and what we do is set up opportunities through classes, through the Discourses, through the taped seminars, so that people can continue partaking of the teachings in various ways.

We've also been looking at how to make the teachings available to people beyond the core group [of current members], but not so that it interferes or distracts from somebody having an essentially spiritual contact. How do we make the teachings available? Is it a pure form of delivery? Is it a clear messenger? I look at myself. I'm a messenger. J-R is a messenger. Other ministers are messengers, to greater or lesser degrees. And then the Discourses are messengers. The classes are messengers. Those are all part of delivering the information. And we're constantly working on, How do we do that in the best way so that people have as pure, clear, and direct contact as we can? What is the essential teaching here, and how do you partake of it?

I look at someone like Woody Guthrie or Willie Nelson — you know, somebody who pays their dues. Why would they sing for years and years, constantly having to hustle, and then one day everybody wants to hear their music and they're buying their records by the millions? What happened? Did the sound of their voice shift or something else happen? What I see is that something about who they are shifted. That's what I see more than anything. It wasn't that their talent suddenly took this leap. It's more like that the context of their life shifted, and people heard them. It's like their soul, their spirit, who they are, started coming out through the music.

There are plenty of examples of singers where people can say, "Well, they don't have a particularly good voice," Joe Cocker, you know, or other people. It's almost like you can listen and be disturbed by it. But there's something else that comes through. They sing with their heart, their presence, and that's what makes the difference. And I have a sense there's something like that in what we're doing. Whatever is not allowing the teachings to transmit on a mass scale where people really respond to it in large numbers isn't so much about their content.

And it's not going to be, "Oh, yeah, the day we started doing this methodology, then everybody got what we were doing and really responded in huge numbers." Because we've done a lot of things to — let's call it market ourselves — to make MSIA presentable. For the most part, when we try to do things according to a technique, it's worse. If we try to advertise or promote ourselves, in some way it turns people off. If we just say, "Here we are, here's what we're doing," that seems to be the best method. To encourage people to trust themselves in their own experience, that's still the best way for people to have the contact. A person has their own experience, shares their experience in some way, and the other person picks up on it and starts responding to it.

I got involved in the *Life 101* series. I used to be confounded that J-R has very good practical information that doesn't have to be about a religious practice. He's got so much good common sense, and he has a way of relating it that's very personable — a lot of anecdotes, a lot of personal experiences. Why don't people respond to them, just on that level? *Life 101* was another experiment. Other people had come forward in an attempt to take the information and put it into a form that people respond to. And then when it happened that J-R was suddenly a bestselling author, to me it was like, "Well, here we are." I don't have an answer as to why then and not earlier. It clicked. It worked. It struck a chord that people responded to.

Lewis: But it really didn't bring that many new people into MSIA.

John Morton: This is true. One of the things we do is make information available. If everybody lived by the set of principles taught in MSIA, we'd have a really wonderful world. I look at the basic teachings about living in the world and I say, "I can't find a finer set of just straightforward, practical, everyday teaching information." Not that I've done exhaustive research, but I've read a lot of sources. I keep coming back because this is the one I resonate with.

Lewis: What I sense — and I've said this to other people so I may as well say it to you guys, too — is a Movement-wide ambivalence about growth. There's the desire to keep the intimacy of the early days, and there's also the desire to reach out further. I sense this at all levels of the organization. It's as if at an energetic level there's an ambivalence. It's almost like if you were to grow and expand, you would have to give therapy to the whole organization. This is not to say that you should grow. Maybe that would dilute whatever there is here so much that it would become just so much blah-blah-blah. Maybe it shouldn't grow. But at present, because of this energetic thing, it's like no matter what you do you're going to remain the same size.

When I talked to Paul Kaye, he said, "As president of MSIA, I really want to see it grow and grow and grow." But he also said, "As a personal, individual seeker after soul consciousness, I don't care." Now when the president of an organization can make that kind of statement, it really says something. And it's not just Paul, it's everybody.

J-R: It's hard to call us aggressive about recruiting members when you see the prevailing attitude. It's incongruent when people say, "Well, you have secret recruiting things." We say, "No, we don't; we don't have any." We're a group of notorious nonjoiners. Everybody maintains their own individuality.

John Morton: My experience, and I consider that John-Roger says something quite similar to this, is that this is something that's being done from the Spirit. We don't have much of a position, and we don't have issues, because that's not really how we function. Then again, on a practical level we organize and we identify certain principles and we have guidelines, but the guidelines don't have teeth. We're not enforcers. We don't exile people from the Church because they have blasphemed or anything like that. It's like we don't take those kinds of issues.

When people attack us, it's like attacking a phantom. We might as well laugh. You could tear this body from limb to limb, but you're not going to get at the source because it's not this body. And it's not J-R's body. So for someone to go, "Well, all you have to do is wipe out John-Roger and John Morton, then it will fall apart," is silly. I couldn't tell you whether the organization itself would survive, because it's really not meant to survive any longer than it's useful. There was a day not so long ago when it didn't exist, because it wasn't useful. Then a day arrived when it started becoming useful to organize and we organized, and we have run into all of the anguish and the friction that comes from being an organization. An organization has a certain kind of a nature that's like a beast. It's ugly, in the sense that it is misrepresentational. In other words, the organization does things that misrepresent the Spirit. Something gets lost in the translation [from the Spirit to the physical level]. But, in order for us to be able to accomplish anything, we have to express through an organization.

Lewis: There's another issue that impinges on this question that may be a key here. When sociologists of religion classify religious groups, as dubious an enterprise as that is, they distinguish groups as world-affirming and world-denying. World-denying meaning a movement that is more focused on the salvation of individual souls, and world-affirming is more focused on transforming the planet.

J-R: Personally, I think that's baloney. You can transcend your soul right here, in this physical world, and be in an enlightened state of consciousness and deny nothing. See, MSIA doesn't fit into the sociological matrix of how you're defining groups. There's a reason why most of the membership in MSIA are in the Spirit. They're only here to get something that kicks them off, like a pizeostarter for a flame. They come in and they go, "Oh, wow! Oh, I got it." They don't need to come back again.

Other parts of the interview relevant to the question of the future of MSIA dealt with such issues as to what might happen once John Morton became sole spiritual leader of the organization. One line of speculation I had entertained was that perhaps John's leadership style would be more suited to a large organization than J-R's, so that real growth in size might not occur until after John-Roger had passed on. This line of questioning was met with the same basic response I received throughout the entire interview, namely that MSIA just does what it does and, if the Spirit wants it to grow larger, then fine. If the Spirit wants it to remain the same size, fine. And even if the Spirit wants the organization to shrink, then that would be okay too.

While this response may seem like the final answer to the question about MSIA's prospects for future growth, I interviewed one longtime member during the final stage of this research project whose observations seemed to throw light on the question at a whole new level. Her remarks seemed the appropriate note on which to end this study:

> *The Movement isn't for everyone because there's no one in the organization who you can make responsible for your faults and failings. There's no one you can go to who's going to solve it for you. There's no grading system. There's no discipline, in the sense of requiring*

you to do certain things and to be a certain way in order to be in the Movement — it's absolutely a matter of taking responsibility and being self-motivating.

I don't know how many people can get excited about something like that. I think if a lot more people became interested in MSIA, it would be because something had changed in our social consciousness so that more and more people would want to take responsibility for their own lives — so that they wanted to not just talk it, but to walk it in their everyday lives, and really hold themselves accountable for their choices and for the lives they had built.

I also think that as we in the organization start to come into a sense of solidity in ourselves — a sense of trust in our own truth — that we will begin to reach out more into the world and share. As we are more out in the world and people like me are just standing in quiet ways, doing service in the world, people might come to the Movement in that way — NOT to become a devotee of a teacher, but to come to a discipline, one that has a lot of different tools for self-transformation. I think more people might come to MSIA in this way.

ABOUT THE AUTHOR

Professor James R. Lewis is Chairperson of the Department of Religious Studies at the World University of America. He has an extensive background in the academic study of religion and is a world-recognized authority on controversial religious movements. He publishes and edits a scholarly journal on non-traditional religions. He also directs AWARE, an organization devoted to investigating current religious controversies.

Many of Professor Lewis's publications reflect his wide-ranging interest in non-traditional religions. He is, for example, the general editor of the forthcoming *Encyclopedia of New Religions* (soon to be published by Prometheus Books). He is the author/editor of academic anthologies on the Branch Davidians (Rowman & Littlefield) and on the New Age movement (SUNY Press). The State University of New York (SUNY) Press has also published his *The Gods Have Landed: New Religions From Other Worlds* and his *Magical Religions and Modern Witchcraft*.

Professor Lewis's *Astrology Encyclopedia* (Gale Research/Visible Ink Press) received American Library Association and New York Public Library awards. He has also written the *Encyclopedia of Afterlife Beliefs and Phenomena*, the *Dream Encyclopedia*, *Alien Images: Popular Culture and UFOS*, *Modern Witchcraft A to Z* and *Angels A to Z*. Finally, he has been a consultant for *Eastern Mysteries* (Time-Life Books), and for such popular TV Specials as "Ancient Prophecies."

ADDITIONAL STUDY AND RESOURCE MATERIALS

An educator and minister by profession, John-Roger continues to transform the lives of many by educating them in the wisdom of the spiritual heart. If you've enjoyed this book, you may want to explore and delve more deeply into John-Roger's teachings through the Movement of Spiritual Inner Awareness. From among his vast body of work, we have selected the following for your consideration.

Soul Awareness Discourses—A Home Study Course for Your Spiritual Growth
The heart of John-Roger's teachings, Soul Awareness Discourses provide a structured and methodical approach to gaining greater awareness of ourselves and our relationship to the world and to God. Each year's study course contains twelve lessons, one for each month. Discourses offer a wealth of practical keys to more successful living. Even more, they provide keys to the greater spiritual knowledge and awareness of the Soul.
$100 one-year subscription
To order call MSIA at 323/737-4055

Soul Awareness Tape Club Series
This audio tape-a-month club provides members with a new John-Roger talk every month on a variety of topics ranging from practical living to spiritual upliftment. In addition, members of the SAT Club may purchase previous SAT releases.
$100 one-year subscription
To order call MSIA at 323/737-4055

Spiritual Warrior: The Art of Spiritual Living by John-Roger
This book is essential for every person who wants to integrate his or her spiritual and material lives and make them both work. A practical guide to finding greater meaning in everyday life, this revolutionary approach puts us firmly on the higher road to health, wealth and happiness; prosperity, abundance and riches; loving, caring, sharing and touching. This book is a #1 *Los Angeles Times* Healthy Bestseller.
ISBN 0-914829-36-X
$20 hardcover
Available in bookstores everywhere

The Tao of Spirit by John-Roger
Eighty-one contemplative passages that can help you let go of this world and return to the stillness within. Timeless wisdom you can live by.
ISBN 0-914829-33-5
$15 hardcover
Available in bookstores everywhere

Forgiveness: The Key to the Kingdom by John-Roger
How to walk under grace and open up to the Divine. A profound truth explained clearly and simply, touching the heart and healing all things.
ISBN 0-914829-34-3
$12.50 softcover

Walking With the Lord by John-Roger
A beautiful book about spiritual exercises—what they are,
how to do them, and inspiration for your inner spiritual
journey.
ISBN 0-914829-30-0
$12.50 softcover
Available in bookstores everywhere

The Way Out Book by John-Roger
A practical guide to spirituality—to living life more fully,
learning from all your experiences, and becoming more aware
of your spiritual nature. Packed with great and usable
information.
ISBN 0-914829-23-8
$5 softcover
Available in bookstores everywhere

The Two Processes of the Mind: Attitude and Altitude
An excellent introduction to the basic ideas of MSIA: checking
things out, the levels of consciousness, spiritual exercises,
moving beyond the mind to the wisdom of the Soul, and much
more.
$10 audiotape
To order call MSIA at 323/737-4055

The Light, The Truth, and The Way
A classic seminar recorded by John-Roger in 1971, presenting
the basic teachings of the Traveler.
$10 audiotape
To order call MSIA at 323/737-4055

New Day Herald
MSIA's own bi-monthly publication which contains articles by John-Roger and John Morton as well as other informative pieces and a listing of MSIA events around the world.
A one-year subscription is free upon request. Call MSIA at 323/737-4055.

Loving Each Day
A daily e-mail message from MSIA that contains an uplifting quote or passage from John-Roger or John Morton, intended to inspire the reader and give them pause to reflect on the Spirit within. Loving Each Day is available in three languages daily—English, Spanish, and French.
A subscription is free upon request.
To subscribe, please visit the web site www.msia.org

To order any of the items listed above, to learn about MSIA events in your local area, or to request a catalog for a wider selection of study materials, please contact MSIA.

MSIA®
P.O. Box 513935
Los Angeles, CA 90051-1935
323/737-4055
soul@msia.org
www.msia.org